SHAMANISM

Personal Quests of Communion with Nature and Creation

Enjoy these other books in the Common Sentience series:

ANCESTORS: *Divine Remembrances of Lineage, Relations and Sacred Sites*

ANGELS: *Personal Encounters with Divine Beings of Light*

ANIMALS: *Personal Tales of Encounters with Spirit Animals*

ASCENSION: *Divine Stories of Awakening the Whole and Holy Being Within*

GUIDES: *Mystical Connections to Soul Guides and Divine Teachers*

MEDITATION: *Intimate Experiences with the Divine through Contemplative Practices*

NATURE: *Divine Experiences with Trees, Plants, Stones and Landscapes*

SOUND: *Profound Experiences with Chanting, Toning, Music and Healing Frequencies*

Learn more at sacredstories.com.

SHAMANISM

Personal Quests of Communion with Nature and Creation

Featuring

OSCAR MIRO-QUESADA

Copyright © 2022 All rights reserved.

This book or part thereof may not be reproduced in any form, stored in a retrieval system, or transmitted in any form by any means-electronic, mechanical, photocopy, recording, or otherwise without prior written permission of the publisher, except as provided by United States of America copyright law.

The information provided in this book is designed to provide helpful information on the subjects discussed. This book is not meant to be used, nor should it be used, to diagnose or treat any medical condition. The author and publisher are not responsible for any specific health needs that may require medical supervision and are not liable for any damages or negative consequences from any treatment, action, application, or preparation, to any person reading or following the information in this book.

References are provided for information purposes only and do not constitute endorsement of any individuals, websites, or other sources. In the event you use any of the information in this book for yourself, the author and the publisher assume no responsibility for your actions.

Books may be purchased through booksellers or by contacting Sacred Stories Publishing.

Shamanism: Personal Quests of Communion with Nature and Creation
Oscar Miro-Quesada

Print ISBN: 978-1-958921-00-5
EBook ISBN: 978-1-958921-04-3

Library of Congress Control Number: 2022944987

Published by Sacred Stories Publishing, Fort Lauderdale, FL USA

CONTENTS

PART ONE: UNDERSTANDING SHAMANISM

The Shamanic Call 5
A Noble Death 13
Awakening Our Shamanic Soul 23
The Cosmic Abode 31
Honoring All Our Relations 43
As Within, So Without 47

PART TWO: PERSONAL QUESTS OF COMMUNION WITH NATURE AND CREATION

From Asthma to Apotheosis *Oscar Miro-Quesada* 57
A River Happening *Allison Kenny* 63
Claiming Power from Our Past *David Jordan* 69
Soul to Soul Siblings *Kathy Guidi* 71
Siwa and the Amazigh Women *Annette Assmy* 75
The Bones of My Heart *Adele Goodwin Keleher* 81
My Shamanic Healing *Debbie Irvine, MCoun* 87
She Will Dream Through Us *Victoria Hanchin* 93
Alaskan Bliss *Deborah Shining Star* 97
Honoring the Ancestors *Debra Kelly* 101
A Healing Call at a Mohawk Village *Ysette Roces Guevara, Ph.D.* 105
Journey to the Shuar *Dr. Bonnie McLean* 109
The House of the Dancing Spirits *Judy Lemon* 113
Rendezvous with Spirit *June Konopka* 117
Love Casts Out Fear *William O. Fogarty* 123

Two Miracles in One Miraculous Day *Diane E. Broitman* 129
Singing with Gaia *Anastasia Michelle* 133
Discovering the Robe Washer *Temple Hayes* 137
When Stones Speak *Robin Blaire Harman* 141
Snakeskins and Rabbit Tales *Rev. Stephanie Red Feather, Ph.D.* 145
The Snow Bunting *Agustina Thorgilsson* 151
The Dream Calling *Mona Rain* 155
The Call to Heal *Rodney Garcia, M.D.* 159
Travels Behind the Veil *Armine Bonn* 163
Eternity *Nancy E. Brown* 169
Snake Medicine *Michael Bluemoon Riveron* 173
Chrysalis *F. Pieter Lefferts* 179
The Light Storm *Amanda Montoya* 183
How the Power Came *Sharon M. Sirkis* 187
Blessed by Invisibility *Oscar Miro-Quesada* 193

PART THREE: DEEPENING YOUR SHAMANIC CONNECTION

The Shaman's Medicine Way 203
Activating Shamanic States Of Consciousness 215
Keeping The Fire Alive 231
A Path Of Peaceful Living 241

APPENDIX: A CELEBRATION OF OUR SHAMANIC ANIMAL ALLIES ...247
MEET OUR SACRED STORYTELLERS 263
MEET OUR FEATURED AUTHOR 269

PART ONE
Understanding Shamanism

Everyone may regulate and educate his imagination so as to come thereby into contact with spirits, and be taught by them.

— PARACELSUS

THE SHAMANIC CALL

Today's shaman leaves new footprints on paths of psychic awareness and spiritual wisdom that are more than 70,000 years old. Shamanism is a tradition of healing, power, and wisdom that sees all life as interconnected and sacred. The process of shamanic awakening is as vast as the universe itself. Physical and spiritual worlds blend with one another, and the shaman's path lies in attaining a life of harmony with both.

The etymology of the word "shaman" is derived from the Tungusic Siberian word *šamān*, which means "to arouse oneself by heat through fire, to be the master of fire." This arousal is known to shamanic initiates worldwide. The word's secondary meaning is "he or she who speaks to spirits or is possessed by spirit."

The shaman is our world's oldest professional, and shamanism is the profession from which all modern medical doctors and ordained priests descend. The shaman is the original dramatist, musician, artist, intellectual, poet, bard, magician, juggler, folksinger, weatherman, healer, advisor of chiefs and kings, ambassador, trickster-transformer, and culture hero.

Those who hear the shaman's call are known by many different names around the world. They may be called folk healer, witch doctor, curandero,

Part One

curandera, brujo, midwife, hampiq, yatiri, kahuna, wakan, or simply medicine wo/man. Regardless of the name, the shaman's path is one of healing service using human, animal, plant, mineral, and supernatural means. Shamans cure the sick, reveal things hidden in time and space, lead sacred ceremonies and ritual initiations, perform offerings to Mother Earth and Great Spirit, and are the revered bearers of ancient tribal lore.

Shamanism is perhaps the first medicine ever practiced, but it is more than just medicine. Shamanism is a way to see and make sense of the world. Many cultures, in all parts of the globe, operate with shamanistic beliefs. The internal logic of a shamanistic culture is far from simple; as a matter of fact, it is a truly remarkable way to conceptualize reality. Shamanism involves contact with ancestral spirit helpers, magical flight or soul travel, voluntary spirit possession, dreamwork, divination, life-and-death confrontations with daemonic entities, therianthropy or the shapeshifting of humans into animals (and vice versa), visionary trance, altered states of consciousness precipitated by the ingestion of sacramental plant medicines, and last but not least, an extraordinary repertoire of ritual healing arts, ethnobotanical treatment modalities, and earth-honoring ceremonial practices.

In the shamanic worldview, mind and body are inseparable. There is no distinction perceived between physical, psychological, spiritual, and social ills. Even life and death are not seen as separate conditions. Healing, in a native sense, means making a person whole by restoring the health of the body, mind, spirit, and community. Sometimes it means accepting what is. Tribal shamanic societies believe that we are part of the universe and must be in balance with all of Mother Earth and Father Sky in gratitude to Great Spirit; a lack of right relationship leads to a lack of balance. Shamanism can create the awareness necessary for the restorative right action so necessary today.

A shaman is one who develops a personal and intimate relationship with seen and unseen worlds for the purpose of being of service as a healer, to mediate between worlds on behalf of others and community. This relationship is cultivated experientially through self-induced, altered states of consciousness, ritual ceremony, and refined energetic awareness.

Runa Simi—mouth of the people—commonly known as Quechua, is the ancestral language of the Inka Empire, and the *lingua franca* for expressing the subtleties of existence on Earth. Quechua remains a genuine onomatopoeic "living language," spoken by millions of indigenous Andean people today. Consequently, because of its magical, phonetic, imitative correspondence with the sounds of nature, Quechua—much like Vedic Sanskrit—plays a pivotal role in the global awakening of our shamanic soul. I have shared several Quechua terms in this book to give a basic feel for its living medicine power.

SHAMANIC STORYTELLING

Through storytelling, shamanic societies have connected with a sacred manner of knowing that transcends rational discourse and intellectual understanding. For thousands of years, indigenous people communicated primarily through oral tradition, which required the talents of revered storytellers. It also required listeners to open their minds and hearts and to listen with care so that they might, in turn, become keepers of the traditions. For tribal elders, words were magical, invisible, and powerful. Words were medicine; they were the way in which people knew themselves and the wider world around them.

In native stories, songs, dances, prayers, ritual arts, and sacred ceremonial objects, we can experience the unbroken tie of Spirit and know some of the cultural treasures held in heart by our original peoples. We can enter a timelessness where neither age nor chronology has meaning, where time stands still, and we live in the story. Through our delight, we can come

Part One

into ways of knowing beyond that of any noun-based, descriptive, written language.

Shamans often learn their origin stories and medicine by dreaming and being taught by spirits. In the coastal desert, Andean highland, and Amazonian rainforest regions of Peru, a great number of native healers claim they've experienced the creation of the world in their dreamtime. As a matter of fact, my own mentor in traditional *altomisayoq* medicine ways, don Benito Qoriwaman Vargas, often told me that "he was present from the beginning and saw and heard it all." He said he "lived our world's beginning while it occurred in real time, by repeatedly dreaming the same creation story and thus learning it firsthand." Once he had become proficient at living the origin story that he first dreamt, it took him a minimum of four nights to recount it, if asked.

In shamanic societies, the oral storytelling tradition keeps cultural truth alive as surely as food sustains the body. I once heard this truth underscored by San Carlos Apache elder Dale Curtis Miles when he said: "We do not like our stories referred to as myths; our sense of who we are in our worldview are wrapped up in these stories. Even clothing, tools, baskets, and other material culture so important in everyday life, have direct links to the stories of the people."

Based on this understanding, shamanic storytelling is something lived and lived through, a way in which the soul finds itself in life; a form of soul-making that serves to de-literalize consciousness and restore its connection to our primordial and metaphorical cognitive origins. Heartfelt shamanic storytelling is a lived experience fraught with inspirational personal meaning. Such a story can fuel our human evolutionary direction and existential choice by recounting how a particular historical event has been altered by the intervention of the sacred and numinous in the world. In this way, the story serves to spiritualize our human relationship with ordinary dimensions of earthly reality.

In a nutshell, shamanic storytelling is soul-making *par excellence*, a deliteralizing of consciousness and thinning of the veil between the seen and unseen expressions of our Great Originating Mystery. This is why, in preliterate societies, the oral tradition is not memorized but remembered.

Stories are a form of medicine. They have the power to heal and to clarify identity. Stories also unify the community by reinforcing our cultural and spiritual continuity. During traumatic events, indigenous people will use the stories they grew up with to make sense of their lives. Stories tell us that a difficult, painful experience—such as addiction, abuse, or loss—has in it the dormant seeds for transformation. The native philosophy holds that each transformation brings about the necessary teachings and experiences for the next crisis and transformation. The enlightenment process becomes a circle of greater and greater self-awareness as well as awareness of one's place in the universal circle of friends, family, nation, and beyond.

A common understanding among indigenous peoples is that every time you heal someone, you give a piece of yourself away, until at some point, you will need healing yourself. You take something of yourself and give it away, free of charge. You do this because you believe you are connected to everything else. You become aware of yourself as a part of everything. You suffer momentarily so that someone else will not have to.

Among many native people, the "patient" or healee is placed on a chair in the center of a circle surrounded by his or her family, friends, and other trusted persons. Then the native healer or medicine person will often tell those present, "One day, you may possibly need to sit in that chair yourself." This serves as a poignant reminder for those participating in a communal healing circle to never think of themselves as superior to the patient. We are all part of a Great Circle, and a circle has no head or top. I'm fond of reminding all earnest aspirants of initiation into the Great Work that "the first shall be last, and the last shall be first." Jesus reportedly said this during his famed Sermon on the Mount.

Part One

We tell the stories to pass on the insight in a way that allows people to remember who they are—to let them see the shadow without running away. We tell the stories to let people remember that there are always alternatives. We tell the stories and, sometimes, the stories tell us.

OUR DESTINY LIES IN OUR ORIGINS

We once moved through a wilderness where every plant, every rock, and every animal spoke to us, embracing us in its song. Every moment was soul-animated, charged with vitality and heartfelt wonder. As humanity, we found delight in being one with the ebb and flow of this fluid correspondence with the natural world. And so long as we were attentive and appreciative, we remained immersed in nature's abundant spirit. Aware of the stories being told, our shamanic ancestors knew about the interdependency of life. They were viscerally attuned to Mother Earth's dreaming; her evolutionary, cosmic eras; the transformational world cycles; and the tonalities, pulses, and rhythms that make up the wondrously creative Great Sacred Hoop of Life.

Yet they were aware also of the unique separateness of human life. They were careful not to let themselves be fated by the material world and kept alive the languages needed to cultivate this relationship–storytelling, ritual, song, dance, pilgrimage, and the vitally important co-creation and sustenance of nature-venerating sacred community. In these compassionate ways, people flourished, and as children became elders, they shared with every new generation the wisdom of the courtesies that allowed the earth and humanity to co-exist in a sacred trust.

All contemporary shamanic cultures share the vision that our Earth Mother is calling us, her children, back. We are being called back to the age-old and time-proven "native medicine ways" to heal our planet and ourselves. She beckons us so that we may once again walk in balance and reverence upon her sacred ground. If we live our lives, love our families, connect with others, and manage our organizations according to the laws and values of both the seen and unseen worlds, we will heal ourselves and humanity.

Yet, even more than healing, our planet needs loving. We can likely say the same thing about all of us.

A NOBLE DEATH

The path of shamanism is rooted in a transcendent paradox. Every moment, thought, and act, poses a unique opportunity and challenge for transformational growth—but only if we recognize and accept what's present and, paradoxically, tune in to how we can assist and serve what needs to change.

One must live the path to understand it. It excludes no one, and yet includes only those willing to surrender a limited sense of self. Often, that begins with a process of ego-annihilation and the death of one's outmoded way of being in the world. This is known as a *shamanic dismemberment.* I've realized that, after the ego-annihilating intensity of shamanic initiation, once one sets foot on the path, there is no turning back. Authentic shamanic practice expresses itself, inevitably, as both a vocation and avocation—an honoring and fulfilling of our soul's *dharma*—our purpose—and a dedicated form of spiritual *sadhana,* our practice.

This practice can manifest itself as a voluntary course of action in salutary response to the health needs of one's community. Or it might express itself involuntarily, in the form of a radically transformative, visionary encounter with non-ordinary dimensions of reality that is meant to inspire a life of selfless dedication to the species-wide well-being of our Earth Mother.

Whether *dharma* or *sadhana*, any authentic shamanic Earth walk is essentially an expression of our innate, human, evolutionary yearning for meaningful participation in the cosmic dance of Creation's dreaming.

BECOMING A HOLLOW BONE

Becoming a *hollow bone* means being a vessel for the manifestation of spiritual power upon Earth. A shamanic practitioner who is considered a hollow bone is someone who has turned their life and will over to the Divine. Someone thought of as a hollow bone can allow the fullness of healing grace and spiritual wisdom from the Above to flow through them into the Below. Like a hierophant adept at the occult art of theophany—making visible the invisible—a shaman regarded as a hollow bone realizes they are not the source of medicine, but simply an empty, open, transparent conduit and instrument used to fulfill the mandates of Great Spirit. Essentially, the direction of one's curing and healing work establishes the kind of life one must lead.

Frank Fools Crow, who lived from 1890 to 1989, is perhaps the most respected *wicasa wakan*—a holy person—among the Lakota people since his uncle, Nicholas Black Elk. He claims to be a hollow bone is like being a pipeline that connects Wakan Tanka, the Creator, and one's tribal community. That said, Fools Crow would be the first to make clear that his healing power is not his own. The power of Wakan Tanka, "the highest and most holy One," runs through a *wicasa wakan* only to the extent that the person has made themselves into a vessel for that power by becoming humble and unselfish. Although few can heed the call from Spirit to be tribally sanctioned medicine carriers, anyone can, in principle, serve as a hollow bone. Accordingly, any dedicated shamanic healer is called upon to become a clean, empty, pristine, unhindered conduit for Divine grace to find its way into our human world.

SURRENDER TO THE DIVINE

An archetypal pattern at play behind the process of shamanic initiation is intimately connected to the widely popular hero or heroine quest, which has been given literary expression in fables, legends, and great spiritual epics. This cyclical birth, death, and rebirth process involves a deeply transformative experience of personal renewal and unlimited self-discovery. What follows is a five-step, cross-cultural distillation of this universal shamanic sojourn of initiation as a selfless servant of the Divine.

I. SLEEPWALKING

Life is living you instead of you living life. Once you have awakened—as each of you reading this book has—you can never really go back to sleep.

II. THE INITIATORY CRISIS

The spiritual calling to a shamanic life path is exactly like being awakened from a good dream. Try as you might, you cannot return to the same dream. Although predominantly experienced as a radically life-changing, transpersonal crisis or spiritual emergency, the call to shamanic initiation occurs in many forms. Such transformations are commonly fraught with intensely destabilizing personal challenges. This intensely self-transformational experience is known as the "shamanic dismemberment" process.

Akin to the archetypal life, death, and rebirth cycle epitomizing the mythic hero or heroine's sacred quest, shamanic dismemberment necessarily involves profound ego-annihilation, radical identity dissolution, and a complete letting go of one's attachment to any socially conditioned sense of self. It is important to realize that the transformational intensity of psychic or physical dismemberment associated with a shamanic calling depends on how stubborn we have been at resisting the call in the past. Accordingly, some of the most common triggers of shamanic initiatory crises in our postmodern world involve:

- PTSD from war or personal trauma related to childhood abuse
- Identity crisis and psychological depersonalization
- Self-doubt and inner confusion
- Family or environmental chaos
- Life-threatening illness or severe health problems
- Long periods of isolation or incarceration
- Physical or sensory deprivation
- Near-death experiences or non-volitional out-of-body episodes
- UFO close encounters, spirit possession, and unprepared exposure to other anomalous or supernatural phenomena
- Lucid dreams and/or spontaneous, precognitive visions of future events
- Vision quests and sacramental plant ceremonies.

III. THE APPRENTICESHIP PROCESS

Sometimes a teacher selects you. But when you are ready to answer a call, in service to Spirit, a teacher shows up in your life. A period of training and discipline begins in which you learn to become an effective instrument of Divine revelation. This process involves both an inner and outer apprenticeship.

Apprenticeship to the "Seen" or Outer World

- Enter a sacred relationship with an appropriate teacher.
- Learn ceremony, ritual, and healing techniques.
- Understand a mythology and cosmology supportive of your practice.
- Immerse yourself in study and allow change to unfold effortlessly in your life.

Apprenticeship to the "Unseen" or Inner World

- Be attentive to visionary dreams, non-ordinary or altered states of consciousness, and imaginal worlds born of plant spirit-induced trance states.
- Remain open to spiritual guidance and visitation from non-physical teachers.
- Develop the imaginative capacity to engage in magical flight during shamanic journeying to establish sacred relationships—service alliances—with spirit helpers.

Both inner and the outer apprenticeships are vital to the balanced unfolding of the healer's path. Through the outer apprenticeship, the necessary skills, ritual, culturally sanctioned ceremony, and liturgy are transmitted to the student. These are joined with the appropriate immersion into the myths and cosmology of the tradition. The inner apprenticeship involves one's progressively refined energetic relationship to a ceremonial altar ground or ritual healing space, the cultivation and interpretation of visions, spirit visitations and contact, and magical flight. It is vital that the inner work be engaged in fully to "clear the zone," as it were. Without an intensive purification and cultivation of relationship to the inner, the inhabitants of the Unseen Realm will never reveal themselves.

IV. BREAKTHROUGH/ILLUMINATION

Breakthrough occurs when we successfully face our *impedimenta*—our emotional baggage—and fully embrace our shadow aspects and the personal shortcomings we have heretofore denied. We awaken to a shamanic life, death, and rebirth journey of conscious self-transformation.

V. RETURN/REINTEGRATION

The Wounded Healer, now transformed into a shaman sage, reclaims his or her place in society as a servant of the Divine, dedicating their life and will in healing service to the greatest good of All Our Relations and Mother Earth as a whole.

HEEDING THE CALL

For those standing on the precipice of true and enduring personality change, the view is everywhere and always the same. To the frightened, aboriginal fourteen-year-old thrust by his elders into the mystery theater of an unfamiliar, wild rainforest habitat; to the young woman-child introduced by a trusted grandmother to her budding female capacities; and to the overwrought corporate executive falling apart under the stress of macabre and irrepressible nightmares, the same sequence of imaginal events unfolds:

- Estrangement from family or tribe and friends
- Grueling ordeal, a solitary odyssey into the cradle of the cosmic mother
- Ego-annihilation or psychic dismemberment
- And finally, rebirth into a new identity and way of being in the world that far surpasses anything previously imagined as possible.

Among aboriginal shamanic societies and most tribal peoples, vivid ritual enactments and ceremonial dramatizations of this cyclical birth, death, and rebirth process are indispensable initiatory opportunities crucial to sustaining their collective ethos—a communal sense of identity.

In cultures where "rites of passage" have become insipid or non-existent, the uninitiated enter phases of personal travail without preparation. In other words, as the co-creators of our current post-modern reality, rather than experiencing intensely transformative, personal progressions supported by a traditionally sanctioned setting, we are now forced to face such personal upheavals alone. These disruptions often appear in the form of disturbingly bizarre dreams, pathological fantasies, or chaotic visions unleashed from the shadowy depths of our collective unconscious. These "demons within" can significantly undermine one's functional waking life, as there is no demarcation into the sacred—no rehearsed or practiced initiation to prompt the transition from a predictable, known world into a shockingly unpredictable, unknown world.

This situation is a set-up for failure, or at least senseless—rather than purposeful—productive, struggle. Only when we completely surrender to the inherent wisdom contained within our Wounded Healer archetype can we integrate the transformational crisis into a lifestyle founded upon a path of gentleness, reverence, and sacred interdependent relationship with the Great Sacred Hoop of Life.

Part One

This process is well-known to the age-old shamanic tribal societies of Eurasia, Africa, the Americas, and elsewhere. For them, an encounter with the wounded healer archetype, replete with initiatory death–rebirth imagery, is the first manifestation of the mystic vocation or shamanic calling that characterizes the individual's potential for marshaling sacred power.

The shamanic slant on personal growth, therefore, is not especially desired or sought-after in a conscious manner. For those who feel its not-so-gentle persuasion, refusing to yield to its beckoning voice might cause pain. It might, potentially, lead to physical, emotional, and psychic deterioration or death. As Dante Alighieri reminds us in his *Divine Comedy*: "He who goes willingly, the fates will lead; he who does not go willingly, the fates will drag along." Hence, it is safe to say that both spontaneous or intentionally ritualized shamanic initiations involve a crisis that leads to a radical personality change, spiritual awakening, and ultimately to the wisdom that leads to and comes from being of service to others and our planet.

Such events occur in the lives of many who are drawn to a path of shamanic service. As previously emphasized, long-term disability, catastrophic illness, recovery from severe addiction, and near-death experiences are among the vehicles that seem to cause the recipients to unhinge their minds and souls from conventional, consensus reality. This allows them to touch upon the non-ordinary and supernatural. For some of us, the wounding is our own psychic pain, part of the richness and texture of our own lives, forming the emotional ties and meaning we establish in our life's work. Either way, the mission is to heal self, others, and our planet, and the tools for doing so are invariably revealed through the experience of mystical, visionary, and other non-ordinary states of consciousness.

Aligned in principle and purpose with these wisdom teachings, we can now confidently decree our willingness to become a hollow bone, an instrument of healing light in Divine partnership with Creation. In doing so, our lives effortlessly hold space for our deaths and rebirths, helping midwife us out of our sticky cocoon of ignorance and giving us refuge for self-transformation and the joyous flowering of our shamanic souls.

AWAKENING OUR SHAMANIC SOUL

*B*ecause everything in nature has its own soul and relationship to humans and other things, shamans have always had a great deal of information to learn anew each time they moved to another environment. Because of their innate adaptability to changing environments, shamanism does not and never did freeze its practitioners or people into a single, dogmatic, magical worldview. That would have prevented them from practical observation and action.

Shamanism has survived, despite cultural differences. Socially, politically, and economically, a great gulf separated the pre-Columbian civilizations such as the Inka, Maya, and Aztec from their European counterparts. We know from the Spanish chroniclers that the professional priests of the Inka in Peru continued to hold the same ideas about the reciprocal relationship between humans, animals, and the spirit world as had their shamanic ancestors. In fact, the pre-conquest shamanic healer continued to flourish alongside the professional priesthood of the urban civilizations.

Shamanism has been called humanity's most ancient form of spirituality. It is a spiritual phenomenon intimately associated with a soul-animated reality. It has persisted across a broad spectrum of beliefs, even where the local religion has changed over time. The gods, goddesses, spirits, legends, and ritual customs associated with shamanism are amazingly similar, no matter the geographical area or social milieu of the practitioner.

In the shamanic cosmology, all phenomena—everything we see, hear, or feel—and every animal, plant, cloud, rock, and ceremonial artifact has a soul. Something that a person from modern society considers an inanimate object, the shaman experiences as a living, sentient being, partaking of consciousness and the ability to communicate. The notion that all things have a soul is known as *animism*. It derives from the Latin word *anima*, meaning soul, which comes from the Greek word *animus*, meaning wind or breath. Amerindian tribal peoples even attribute god-like qualities to certain species of plants, especially their most important food sources and sacramental plant medicines.

TODAY FOR YOU; TOMORROW FOR ME

In this multiverse of animate things, all relationships are governed by the principle of sacred reciprocity—also referred to as the "law of right returns." Known as *Ayni* by Peru's native Quechua-speaking people, this principle is considered a Divine measure of evolutionary equilibrium and a universal, life-stabilizing dynamic that is indispensable to living a balanced life of reverence for Mother Earth and All Our Relations. This quintessential activity of sacred reciprocity not only guides and informs the societal needs and relationships of native people, but also between people and animals, people and plants, people and tribal habitats, and most significantly, among people and ancestrally venerated tutelary spirits.

Within the Andes, a delicate reciprocity means that all things in nature are interdependent, and each is integral to the whole of the universe. Yet this principle is resilient. Harmony and ethos govern the interaction between the many parts of creation. Woven from the multicolored strands of reciprocity, obligation, and respect, this system of communal interchange is *Ayni*. In other words, *Ayni* is both a code of conduct and sense of identity, or *ethos*, and the organizing principle—or *archai*—of the Andean cosmos and shamanic worldview.

From within this socially defining paradigm of action, the actors in a living, vibrant cosmos negotiate balance among its diverse parts through ritual and ceremonial observance. At times elaborate, at times solitary and simple, the performance of *Ayni* infuses and informs all aspects of life upon *Pachamama's* sacrosanct body. The soaring heights of the mountains and the fertile soil of the valleys are continuously acknowledged within its reciprocal laws. In this terrain, every tendency of geography performs a particular role in the survival and well-being of the community and is therefore deeply considered in the rituals of sacred reciprocity.

This interchange regulates all aspects of life and ritual. The reciprocity it embodies forms the key Andean insight into the universal, shamanic cosmos: that all things interconnect, interpenetrate, and interweave, and that the order necessary for harmonious co-existence can only be founded on reciprocal consideration and exchange.

When applied to human relations, eco-agricultural management, spiritual noesis, and religious life, the principle of *Ayni* ensures an integrity of both whole and part among the vast system of relations that is the living world, the *kawsaypacha*. As the means of right relationship, *Ayni* establishes an ordered continuum of interaction and thus promotes well-being through the recognition of *place* and *essential identity*. In other words, by knowing *who one is* and *where one is*, the path of appropriate equilibrium becomes clear.

The word "healing" derives from the Greek word meaning "to become or make whole." To attain wholeness is to become essentially related from within one's place in the cosmic harmony. In essence, maintaining that relationship is the work of *Ayni*.

Woven into the fabric of indigenous life and intimately understood since the dawning of the first peoples, *Ayni* forms the key re-membering of all responsible shamanic practice. It is this re-membering of sacred relationship, in action and intention, that characterizes the ideal of the shamanic healer. This fundamental teaching leads to a life of expressed mutual reciprocity with all facets of the living cosmos and an aware and humble understanding of our place within nature.

Ayni is reinforced by the ethical maxims of *Ama suwa, ama qella, ama yulla*—"don't steal, don't lie, don't be lazy." It directs the healer into an ever-deepening conscious relationship with widening circles of community. Initiated first by the shamanic calling, or "illness," the shamanic student is then awakened to the successive levels of the All That Is, the *T'eqse Muyu*, as conscious integration develops. These form progressive levels of support, as well as realms of service for the shamanic healer's work.

It is easy to forget that the greatest source of suffering in the world is our human estrangement from the sacred dimensions of life. The only thing which will effectively transform our relationship to Mother Earth is a sense of being at one with a sacred cosmos, with a living planet. The indigenous soul exists in all of us. We are all native children born from the miracle that is Gaia.

Some peoples living upon Earth today are closely tied to critical habitat and biodiversity hotspots. They are the stewards not only of habitat, but of the indigenous soul to which we are all heir and which we must reclaim. Laying aside our anger about the past and our fear of the future, we can support each other in exercising a spiritual, compassionate activism. The most powerful force in the world is a resurgent citizens movement. It takes the ability to be fully alive to the present and allows that earthy song to come through us. In uniting to protect the Earth, we inhabit not only the land, but the ground of our being, where past and future fall away and we are enlightened fully, as the soul of the planet.

The reality is that there is no "environment," save in our imaginations. We *are* the Earth. What surrounds us, is us. It shapes us, as we shape it. We must dedicate our dreams, thoughts, words, and actions to the well-being of our species-wide Earth community as a whole and to the work of restoring wonder and a sense of reverence to our world. Drawing from diverse sources of Earth-honoring wisdom, we must inspire each other to walk a graceful path of beauty upon our beloved Mother Earth, celebrating life as a sacred gift and teaching love by the way we live. This is my understanding of the original instructions bestowed upon humankind.

Famed mystics, bona fide mystery school initiates and shamanic adepts the world over understand that the secrets of the universe lie hidden within our human souls, and that the path to their discovery requires the focused, creative use of our imaginative faculties. As shamanic inheritors of the dream of life and the mystery of creation, each of you is a story that the soul of the world tells in continuous conversation between beginning and ending, in the middle waters between life and death. The power of our human imagination to transform the larger social order in which we live is undeniable. We are creativity creating creations gestated through the imaginal dance betwixt matter and spirit, a joyous dance in celebration of their Divine mutuality and unified power for transcending the illusion of polarizing dualities.

THE FIVE AXIOMS OF AN AWAKENED SHAMANIC SOUL

It is common knowledge that all traditional shamanic peoples equate soul with consciousness. They also understand its inherent *a priori* nature and its primacy as the source of all phenomenal manifestations of life. To understand what I mean, simply close your eyes, and call forth in imagination the image of a shamanic power place: a sacred mountain, an elder tribal wisdom keeper, or any ancestrally venerated place or person you've been to or met in the past. Now send yourself on an imaginary flight to visit that same venerated place or spend time with that person.

As you do, the feeling of deep reverence long associated with that place or person becomes experientially imprinted in your consciousness, awakened in your soul, and viscerally integrated at a cellular level in your body—all from that inner vision and "imaginary" journey of sacred visitation. Now also notice, I've deliberately written the word "imaginary" encased in quotations. Doing so personifies its linguistic actuality as a non-physical vehicle for freeing our minds from bodily encapsulation—as an instrument of our highest intelligence in service of our innate human capacity for extending consciousness beyond the confines of material existence.

As a matter of fact, the word imaginary derives from the Latin term *imago*, which literally translates as either "an image of the Self," "the reflection of one's Self," or "a soul's imagery as Self." Thus, image and imagery are at the heart of what we call the imaginary, and our ever-evolving soul experienced in Self-consciousness stems from this kind of imagination. When we understand that we can bring forth these images and awaken our soul as consciousness, we understand that consciousness both structures and in-forms matter.

In other words, the soul gives birth to the world of form. Whether tribal or mystical, all teachers of perennial wisdom are in accord about a living soul that fashions our world. The Latin term for the soul animating our world is *Anima Mundi*. This is the living Being that is behind all material form, from a blade of grass to a spiral galaxy. We understand that *consciousness begets matter*. This has been amply demonstrated, not only theoretically but in experimental physics. Anything that is observed is transformed by the observer.

We also understand that *language begets reality,* meaning that the consensus reality we speak about in terms of what is valuable for a people and that which we need to survive is all based on a shared language. Aware that soul and consciousness are the same causative phenomenon behind the world, it stands to reason that the words we use give expression to our choices about the world that we want. When used in shamanic ritual, our spoken word and the phenomena of language itself activates the medicine power of soul in ourselves, others, stones, plants, animals, ceremonial power objects, spirits, or the entire world. Through heartfelt shamanic ritual, we learn to honor the primacy of soul in relationship to our lives and the natural world. Therefore, *ritual begets relationship.* The hoop of kinship contained in those rituals becomes family, and these rituals are extraordinary in their power to bring wholeness into one's life.

When we acknowledge that ritual begets relationship, we are already aware that the natural world is the place where we are going to receive guidance about what our human purpose is—because *nature begets purpose.* And finally, when we realize the deep love that Creation, our cosmic mother, has for the unfathomable diversity and magic of her dreaming ways, it becomes easy to grasp the fifth axiom of a universally awakened shamanic soul: *love begets life.*

Therefore, trusting soul is at the crux of any shamanic initiate's willingness to receive a bestowal of metahuman abilities in alignment with a higher spiritual purpose on this earth. From the perspective of universal shamanic body of knowledge, it is equally important to understand the purpose for using the *begets* rather than "structures" as a transitive verb for illuminating the living spirit behind these five axioms. The reason is that the word "begets" implies an engendering or "bringing into being" of something that was not yet in existence. It implicates a birthing of sorts and playing a generative role in the emergence of certain conditions and circumstances.

To recapitulate, the five shamanic principles are:

1. Consciousness begets matter
2. Language begets reality
3. Ritual begets relationship
4. Nature begets purpose
5. Love begets life

Adhering to these five axioms guarantees a wisely soul-awakened and empowered path of shamanic service to the Great Work. Moreover, these simple words represent a sublime gift of perennial wisdom applicable to humans and all living creatures on Earth. The five axioms clearly illuminate that *love of nature and ritual is the language of consciousness,* and that we are to celebrate the gift of earthly *life as a purposeful relationship with the reality of matter.*

As we embrace a path of sacred reciprocity and deepen our adherence to living a balanced life founded upon the principle of *Ayni*, a limitless opportunity of encounter and cooperation with ancestral shamanic spirit helpers is made manifest in our lives. Moreover, having traversed a vast, soul-animated universal field of shamanic dreaming, we now stand prepared to embrace the imaginal beauty and spiritual majesty of a living, sentient, and ever-evolving cosmos.

THE COSMIC ABODE

*A*n almost cosmopolitan-held concept of shamanic practice delves into what are referred to as the "three worlds": the upper, middle, and lower—or inner—worlds. These are known in Andean pre-Columbian cosmology as *hanaqpacha, kaypacha,* and *ukhupacha,* respectively. Interestingly, these three worlds have a corresponding framework with some schools of thought of modern psychology: the transpersonal-supraconscious psyche, the interpersonal-conscious psyche, and intrapersonal-unconscious psyche, which together fashion the lived dimensions of human experience.

Central to the embodied practice of Universal Shamanism is the experience that the universe is an inherently animated and living world. In the Andean cosmovision, all things are recognized to live within a *pacha*. *Pacha* is itself a dynamic concept, reflecting the typical Andean sensitivity to the multidimensional nature of existence. As a word, *pacha* may designate a period of time, a location in space, a world, and even the soil itself. Like most of the world's tribal cosmologies, Andean cosmology rests on a vision of a three-fold division of the universe, three pachas: the *Hanaqpacha,* the *Kaypacha,* and the *Ukhupacha.*

Each of these refers to a distinct location within the mythic, daimonic, and physical universe, complete with its own unique characteristics, inhabitants, and "flavor." While each of these realms embodies specific dimensional needs within Creation's overall evolutionary agenda, there exists a deeply refined and intricate interconnection between all *pachas* which is, once again, governed by the universal principle of *Ayni*—or the Law of Right Returns.

While the following makes use of the distinctions of environment for purposes of clarity, it is best to say that the worlds interpenetrate. As their inhabitants travel across the boundaries, there is a fluid interaction between the spaces known as *pachas*. More precisely, the relationship is particularly acute between the *Ukhupacha* and the *Kaypacha*, as it is between the *Kaypacha* and the *Hanaqpacha*. The *Ukhupacha* and the *Hanaqpacha*, on the other hand, do not generally intersect.

What are the "three worlds" from the Andean shamanic perspective, and what do they have to do with personal transformation when it comes to one's initiation into Universal Shamanism? A short overview of these worlds will serve as a primer to shamanic understandings of personal transformations and repositories of wisdom. The spiritual dynamics and spirit denizens of these realms are remarkably like all shamanic tribal societies worldwide— another testament to the universality of shamanism as a truly perennial wisdom path.

HANAQPACHA – THE UPPER WORLD

The *Hanaqpacha* is the celestial realm of the most elevated aspects of Nature and Soul, the luminous realm of pure spirit and Divine purpose, of wisdom and guidance, symbolized by the tutelary animal guide, *Kuntur*—the Condor. It is that place often described as the "heavens," in which superior spiritual tutelage and cosmic consciousness both reside and may be experienced.

In the Andean cosmological conception, the *Hanaqpacha* is a supreme synthesis of the adopted Christian pantheon with the original, indigenous understanding of deity.

As the supra or transcendent world, the *Hanaqpacha* contains archetypal elements of Godhead and Creation that thereafter become manifestly embodied in the *Kaypacha* according to the flow of *kamay*, or creative power. The route of *kamay* is traced from the heavens to the terrestrial. In this way, the *Hanaqpacha* bears the seeds that shall fruit in the *Kaypacha* and provides the spiritual nourishment that sustains all life.

Tradition reveals the *Hanaqpacha* as a multiform world expressive of elevated consciousness and spiritual comprehension, while being the realm in which a soul experiences its highest development. Cross-culturally, the *Hanaqpacha* contains humanity's most refined aspirations and superior apperceptions of spiritual truth as the repository for the laws and principles that guide creation.

The higher emotions, such as love and compassion, have their sustaining roots in the *Hanaqpacha*, which above all, holds the template for dedicated service to the many dimensions of life. Connection with its inspiration is necessary to maintain a higher life of balance, creativity, and service. However, over-exposure—for example, through sustained, premature contact—can lead the human ego to a kind of burn-out in which the personality and the soul's focus in the middle world, the *Kaypacha*, become disoriented and weak. With practice, the spiritual aspirant can draw and integrate ever-increasing amounts of attunement with this highest world.

KAYPACHA – THE MIDDLE WORLD

The *Kaypacha* is the principal focus of humanity's attention, symbolized by the tutelary animal guide *Choquechinchay*—the puma. For us as souls, the

Middle World is the center of our incarnation; for us as people, it is the place where the trajectory of our physical lives is realized. The phenomenological immediacy of the *Kaypacha* imparts to it both great possibility for fulfillment and great potential for suffering. It can derail us with the vicissitudes of materiality. It can captivate, overpower, or overwhelm our spiritual equilibrium if we become entranced by its physical form and forget that this is just one of the dimensions in which we operate. At the same time, there is enormous potential for growth when the spiritual life is harmonized within the *Kaypacha*.

The *Kaypacha* is the immediate realm of experience, and as such faithfully reflects the inner condition of its occupants. As the prime stage for the unfolding drama of consciousness, the *Kaypacha* presents to all the opportunity to experience certain karmic lessons and consequently develop the ability to embody both creativity and love. One is offered the occasion to refine the capacity for love against the harsh measures of physical life. Esoterically, the *Kaypacha* is a powerful teacher, providing a palpable space for negotiating karmic experiences and integrating the principles of *munay* and *Ayni*—love and reciprocity—which are essential to progress. These Quechua words, *munay* and *Ayni*, embody integral parts of shamanic practices to create right relationships. A sacred relationship with self, others, and all life on this planet and beyond, seen and unseen, is at the heart of the shamanic worldview, evident especially within the Peruvian shamanic *curanderismo* and *paqokuna* traditions.

Our current western culture relationship with the planet is almost devoid of *Ayni*. Once we restore this, our sacred relationships will flourish and what we need to live will come to us through the right actions we take.

As alluded to earlier, the ability to hold both opposition and paradox in balance is a vital skill well-mastered in the *Kaypacha*. Since the *Kaypacha* is experienced through the duality of physical and spiritual manifestation, it provides an ideal, though challenging, arena for growth. The direct and confronting presence of physical existence—with the drastic immediacy of its cycles of life, death, and the needs of survival—offers a depth of incarnational wisdom not easily attained in less challenging environments.

It is not without reason that the jaguar and the puma have, since the greatest antiquity, been indelibly related with the nature of life in the *Kaypacha*. As the fiercest predator of Andean peoples, having the power to take human life in a rapturous instant, the jaguar—in exchange as its *Ayni*—offers profound teaching to humanity. To have been devoured by a puma is referred to in Quechua as *pumasqa*, indicating the sense of having been incorporated into the being of the puma by that curious past participle, *-sqa*. Alternatively, it is to be "puma-ed."

Peruvian mythology says that all things earthly have their archetypal source in that liminal realm of stars between the *Hanaqpacha* and the *Kaypacha*, known as the *Hananpacha*. Through this vast net of stars pours the vital power that nourishes their expression in the living world of the *Kaypacha*.

UKHUPACHA – THE LOWER/INNER WORLD

The *Ukhupacha* is often seen as the interior world of emotion and subconscious forces. It is the inner or lower world of soul-making, the realm of shadows and primal consciousness symbolized by *Amaru* or serpent. It is the highly dynamic realm of Soul, and the source of the inner, generative processes of life. The word *ukhu* marks that which stands beyond the boundary of the *Kaypacha*–that which lies underneath the limit of the soil and skin. The *Ukhupacha* also refers to the interior biological space, the region beyond the reaches of the physical eye where the vital processes of life take place, finding their transformations exhibited in exterior growth. Deep mechanisms of nourishment occur in geologic phenomena, the cycles of decay and nutriment, and the chemical assimilations of plants—and in the ancient, ancestral presence of the dead, who guard these inner reaches with their unquestionable and ubiquitous presence.

In a place where the only light comes from within, the mysteries of the *Ukhupacha* are attainable only to consciousness itself. Within the profound, psychic depths of this realm, life is sustained by the labor of those to whom it is home—the many forms of non-human consciousness that are its inhabitants. Together with mechanisms of life—those of a biological, geological, and psychic kind—the *Ukhupacha* provides the essential ground from which the fluorescence of form so characteristic of the *Kaypacha* can grow.

The growth made possible by the *Ukhupacha* extends to the embodied and unembodied elements of nature. In other words, it is not only the soil for the experience of physical form, but also the essential realm for the growth of the soul, whose unfolding takes place largely through the incorporation of itself in the *Ukhupacha*. It is the gathering up of itself from these inner realms that communicates to the soul its expansive unfolding of personal wisdom. As the retrieval of a net from the sea, the soul draws its vitality in great part from the veracity of its relationship with the interior and is marked by the quality of its yield.

The *Ukhupacha* contains powerfully charged, emotional states and symbols, as well as those psychic aspects that have been repressed or ignored by humanity. It is therefore a place of some darkness, though only to individuals who have not integrated their own shadow. Healing practices enable the individual to circumvent and gain protection from any further harmful influence of *Ukhupacha* forces and beings.

The *Ukhupacha* most resembles a mirror in that it accurately and faithfully reflects the inner condition of the soul with intense rapidity. Thus, it is an essential key to self-transformation and healing, as its depths contain those disowned aspects of the soul whose absence keep it in ignorance and fear. The *Ukhupacha* commonly forms the core of shamanic journeys because of its psycho-spiritual depth and power, in addition to its connection with the processes of death. *Ukhupacha* initiation and adeptness become the ground through which true shamanic self-knowledge and wisdom are harnessed.

To fear the *Ukhupacha* is to disempower the self and remain in a state of delusion and projection, which only further feeds the unconscious expressions of our repressed and denied selves within the world. If we fear the *Ukhupacha*, refusing to become knowledgeable of its depths, it inevitably acts through us. We must, instead, learn to master our own inner darkness and express this mastery through the enlightened use of *Ukhupacha* energies. If our relationship to the *Ukhupacha* has not been cleansed, we can hardly experience the vital, life-giving forces that reside there.

OUR SOJOURN UPON *PACHAMAMA*

All three worlds are interdependent and in continuous communication. Born into the *Kaypacha*, the shaman can journey into the lower world through caves and openings into the Earth, following underground streams or by any means of descent. The shaman may also ascend into the upper world by climbing mountain peaks, trees, ladders, crosses, pillars, poles, or ropes. The shaman can also journey through the *Kaypacha* to find lost things, check up on friends and relations, deliver distant healing energy, or visit the future or past. Authentic shamanic journeys through all three worlds eventually require mastering the conscious, out-of-body experience.

Our sojourn upon *Pachamama* can be seen as a game of restoring these three worlds to their original harmony through the dynamic union of *Ayni*. This alchemical fusion of the three worlds is the ultimate gift we can offer for the gift of life. When seen cross-culturally, it is the end to which all higher practices of shamanic work are oriented. It yields balance, soul growth, service, and transformation as vocation. Transformation requires self-awareness, which requires taking an inventory of self and remaining open to discovering parts and places within that are simply not attended to, due to our overreliance on cognitive, waking consciousness.

The consciousness we bring into the world ripples out far and wide across the *Kaypacha*, high into the *Hanaqpacha*, and deep within the *Ukhupacha*. It has the potential to harmonize all three worlds, allowing the lightning bolt of mystical illumination that embodies creativity, creating creation as a bestowal of trust in us from the Creator—*Illa Teqsemuyu Taytanchis Wiraqocha Pachakamaq*—to be manifest. In the Andean shamanic way, this is known as *growing corn and potatoes*. That means as we put ourselves into action in the world to nurture self and others, we simultaneously nurture the cosmos. We do this by allowing both light and shadow to have equal presence in the revelation of self as other, and other as self.

In similar fashion, when we talk about dreaming something into fruition, we are entering into a place where our sleeping dream, our daydream or reverie, and our waking dream—which we often call the everyday—becomes seamless. So, the elements of our sleeping dream, our waking dream, and our daydreaming, or reverie, all begin to experientially merge into one synchronistic flow of shamanic consciousness in our lives. At that point, we know we are living our medicine. Then we will manifest a reality in which we are no longer victims. Instead, we will show up as adept shamanic volunteers capable of owning our power to beneficently influence life circumstances.

It is important to understand that these *pachas*, these three worlds, are repositories of great power and energy. The only reason we are not integrating all three of them and receiving our guidance solely from the *Hanaqpacha*, the upper realm, is because we lack imagination—not will, not capability, but imagination. Sadly, the excessive thinking of an undisciplined mind armors some people who are brilliant in their cognitive abilities and intellect, but who deny the virtue, value, and power of imagination.

TIMELESS PORTALS OF SPIRITUAL POWER

Ancestral places of spiritual power and venerated ceremonial temple sites function much like the hyperspace portals and interdimensional wormholes spoken about in applied theoretical cosmology. They are a concentrated harnessing of sufficient energy from the stars' cosmic sources which causes the electromagnetic and gravitational warping of space-time into a horizon event singularity. Both their design and construction are founded upon a highly advanced knowledge (i.e., hermetic wisdom corpus) and applied ritual mastery of imitative magic.

Such places enable all heartfelt pilgrims gathered upon their ancestrally consecrated maiden ground access to multiple dimensions of being. They help us understand our own immortal selves through a direct experience of the sacred in our lives. They are natural landscape shrines upon which all existing temple sites, ceremonial spaces, and traditionally sanctioned places of visioning, healing, and shamanic initiation are located.

Our ancestors, the original creators of such earthly sanctuaries, understood they were linked by a terrestrial network consisting of a vast web marked by topographical geoglyphs, ancestral burial mounds, pyramids, oracular centers, and ceremonial temples that functioned like a mirror or "looking glass," predictably reflecting the heavenly movements upon the Earth plane. They help us "re-Member" ourselves as a united planetary culture with a common celestial origin in the Milky Way.

Embodied within the natural landscape design, as well as the human-patterned visionary "architecture" of these sacred sites, during cyclical convergence times between Earth and sky, at specific juncture points or astronomical nadir locations within their template, a "heirophany" occurs—a drawing down of cosmic power from the celestial realms into Mother Earth's bioetheric matrix or "ceque body."

Solstices, equinoxes, new and full moons, and other major cyclical periods of astronomical harmonization provide a window of opportunity for humankind to ritually harness and shamanically commune with the spiritual forces of creation. The proper enactment of Earth-honoring ceremonies at ancestral places of power becomes the equivalent of inserting "alchemical acupuncture needles" throughout the meridian pathways in the body—yet on a *macro-cosmic scale*.

As ceremonial Earth stewardship adepts, our "acupuncture needles" consist of ritual "feedings" (*mihushanku*), shamanically empowered co-creation of stone cairns and dolemens (*apachetas / ushnu-sucancos*), consecrated offerings *(haywa despachos)* to the Spirit World at ancient places of worship (*Wakas*) and revered pilgrimage destinations such as mountain shrines (*apus*) and sacred bodies of water (*Mamacochas*). This Great Work allows us to access and transmit benevolent energetic fields ("healing ripples") of transformation into our planetary ceque system—Gaia's geomagnetic grid and stellar bio-etheric web. In essence, this ceremonial "unblocking" and trans-dimensional activation of *Pachamama's allpakawsay* (vital life force or planetary *Qi*) has been proven to empower the emergence of loving eco-spiritual awareness (*Ecosapience*) throughout the world as our most valuable legacy to the Seven Generations.

COMMUNING WITH OUR ANCESTOR'S SKY WORLD

Most ancestral wisdom traditions refer to the "sky world" as a place of human origin and spiritual instruction that play a crucial role in sustaining the cultural identity of Earth's Original Peoples. Whether disclosed in writing through Sumerian cuneiform, Egyptian hieroglyphics, or Sanskrit epics—or transmitted orally as aboriginal creation stories, myths of origin, and tribal legends, the message is the same. As humans, we are predisposed to experiencing some form of "contact" with the transcendent, through some type of encounter with that which lies vastly beyond the confines of our earthly reality. Such profoundly transformational encounters have influenced the origins of religion, elicited cultural evolution, and sparked a scientific revolution.

It is now evident that within our own *Via Lactea*—the Milky Way—numerous life-sustaining planets exist that have given rise to advanced life species capable of self-reflexive awareness. In other words, much like *Homo Sapiens Sapienza*, these advanced life forms are conscious of themselves in their role as observers as well as the "observed." As humankind, born with such self-awareness, it becomes our co-creative evolutionary duty to seek "contact" with the Universe as a whole. But first we must become adept at knowing ourselves, which requires embarking on the most important interstellar journey of all: going within. And there is no better avenue for engaging contact with our inner universe than through mastery of the shamanic arts.

Such mastery involves expanding our sense of self beyond consensus reality, a tenacious plunge into the unshackling of our illusory encapsulation in 3-D mind-space. Agreed upon by mystics, shamanic masters, and the perennial wisdom teachings of heartfelt gnostic adepts from mythic times and places long forgotten—and in great demand today—the most direct route for accessing otherworldly places is by honoring the imaginal domain of our immortal soul's visionary inner spaces. This conscious realization of self as soul results in a Divine revelation of Self.

Individually, each of us has a memory of such originating perennial wisdom. In universal shamanic cosmology, body and soul, or matter and spirit, are simultaneously both part of each other and separate from each other, much as a tree is part of, and yet separate from, both the Earth and the sky. To make visible what is numinous, Divine, or experienced as ineffable in sanctity, a visible manifestation of Great Spirit is needed. It is only by

Part One

consciously befriending this imaginal multiverse that it is possible to shape-shift your materialized earthly circumstance into an unlimited, spirit-guided, malleable personal opportunity.

HONORING ALL OUR RELATIONS

*S*hamans are standout members of a tribe or community who can see the world of spirits. Rather than being imaginary or outside of reality, the spirits are real. When human affairs are in disarray, crops fail, or illness strikes, the shaman is tasked to right the wrong and restore balance in the other worlds to heal the disruption in this one. He or she must take this journey, often at significant personal risk, making the shamanic adept one of the bravest and most selfless of healers.

The masterful shaman can traverse unseen cosmic dimensions in magical flight. Shamans are the sublime messengers of the gods, goddesses, and tutelary spirits known to their tribal communities. Being adept *psychopomps* or "walkers between the worlds" and retrievers of souls, the traditional shaman never fails to fulfill the Divine will of their chief tribal deity. As fully soul-awakened passersby, born to serve humanity's health needs, I consider the traditionally initiated shaman a sublime incarnation of Boddhisattva consciousness on earth.

The ecstatic visionary trance or altered state of consciousness is central to the shaman's vocation. This has been one of its predominant features since the Upper Paleolithic Era or at least the Middle Stone Age. However, the

Greco-Roman western world developed differently as the new messianic religions of Christianity, Islam, and Judaism took hold. The old faiths and practices based on shamanism were suppressed across Europe and Asia. Shamans were demonized as witches, sorcerers, and frauds, and individual visionary experiences were condemned even before the Spanish Inquisition. Knowledge of healing and techniques for contacting the spirit world, which had served shamans and their followers for thousands of years, were condemned as works of the devil.

Fortunately, pre-Columbian Native Americans were able to preserve their shamanistic heritage precisely because, before Columbus, the new world never underwent the massive religious transformations that swept across the old world. On this side of the Pacific, shamans remained a vital asset to tribal society, spiritual life, and physical and mental well-being.

Accordingly, a shaman is one who develops a personal and intimate relationship with the unseen world for the purpose of being of service as a healer. This relationship is cultivated experientially through self-induced, altered states of consciousness, ritual ceremony, and refined energetic awareness. The shaman's task is to come into right relationship and reverent communion with both the seen physical world of matter and body, and the unseen metaphysical world of spirit and soul, and to mediate between these two worlds on behalf of their community.

Most important, shamanism should not be confused with religion. It is an innately non-dogmatic, spiritual practice grounded in a reverent awareness that all of Creation is animated, conscious, and energetically interdependent.

THE FIVE GUIDING PRINCIPLES OF UNIVERSAL SHAMANISM

- Everything is alive (animation/vitalism). Everything manifests a

physical form from the same animated essence. The shaman attends to this essence.
- Everything is conscious (vigilance/observation). Everything watches us. The world is mirrored within us. The shaman learns to be a visionary observer.
- Everything is interconnected (relationship/reciprocity). Everything responds to and is in interdependent relationship to everything else. The shaman is a mediator of these interconnections and interdependent relationships.
- Everything transforms (movement/change). Matter is a dense form of spirit. Spirit is a subtle form of matter. Everything is in vibrational flux. The shaman is an agent of change.
- Everything responds to focused intention (mindfulness/attentiveness). Clarity of intention and purity of motive are indispensable for all heartfelt shamanic practice. The shaman must thoroughly know him or herself in order to help others.

The magic and power of shamanism is grounded in a set of values and perceptions that extend beyond what we usually consider reality. Traditional shamanic peoples have reverently sought visionary guidance from a soul-animated cosmos permeated by both seen and unseen powers and forces, crucial to the flourishing of species-wide life, on Earth and beyond. Home to ancestral spirit helpers and Divine denizens revered by tribal societies since time immemorial, this deeply sentient shamanic cosmos is equally impregnated with the visibility of Mother Nature's life-regenerative generosity, and the invisibility of Great Spirit's evolutionary imprint upon both seen and unseen dimensions of life. Both are equally undeniable.

All shamanic wisdom keepers teach that we need to honor both to get a true picture of reality. Both seen and unseen worlds are held together, run by, and function according to universal principles, laws, and values. There are physical laws, such as the ordering patterns and cycles in nature, and spiritual laws, such as the inviolate sacredness of all life. Although certain culture-specific shamanic practices may vary in form, indigenous ritual healing arts and magico-religious ceremonies have these twelve core principles in common:

THE TWELVE SACRED LIFE DICTUMS OF UNIVERSAL SHAMANISM

- Spirituality, ritual, and prayer
- Respect for nature
- Hard work and a practical sense of humor
- Veneration of age, ancestral wisdom, and tradition
- Relativity of time
- Non-verbal (telepathic) communication and keen observation
- Composure and patience
- Communal child rearing and extended family
- Autonomy and respect for others
- Sacred reciprocity, generosity, and sharing
- Cooperation and group harmony
- An infallible trust in the Great Originating Mystery's soul-affirming evolutionary purpose in our lives

In essence, shamanic societies teach that how we choose to live determines the life we experience. If we choose to live in harmony, we will experience harmony and joy in our lives. To cultivate an intimate relationship with this larger reality, with this all-inclusive universal presence, is indispensable because the ground rules for The Game of Life, known by our Quechua speaking shamanic ancestors as *Pukllay Kawsay*, are within these principles.

AS WITHIN, SO WITHOUT

Shamanic people experience themselves as being part of the natural world rather than the owners of it. In the shamanic worldview, the universe is divided into several horizontal levels, with an underworld below, the heavens above, and a middle world inhabited by humans, animals, plants, and their respective spirit owners or masters and mistresses. The different cosmic levels are, in turn, connected by a vertical axis known as the *Axis Mundi* or shamanic tree, with its roots in the underworld and its leafy crown in the heavens.

This same idea was expressed in secret urban architecture and in the great civilizations of Mesoamerica and the Andes. While these structures also served as tombs of rulers, destratification of the universe is the essential meaning of the stepped temple platforms or pyramids that annually draw hundreds of thousands of tourists from all over the world. These are sacred mountains whose levels correspond to the worldview of their ancient builders. And there are plenty of examples of the shaman's tree in art and surviving rituals.

Shamans were sometimes the political leaders. They were the recognized masters of the spirits who assisted the shamans on their out-of-body journeys through the layers of the cosmos and taught them their curing songs. They were believed to be able to metamorphose from humans to animals and to shapeshift into various forms. They served as mediators between human beings and revered ancestral spirit helpers. They were prophets of weather at the hunt and with the advent of agriculture, some 8,000 years ago, the harvest. And it was these masters of spirits who preserved and passed on the ancient knowledge handed down from the ancestors and who guarded the spiritual and physical equilibrium of their societies and its members.

Regardless of the various functions and powers attributed to shamans and different cultures, they were almost always respected as the healers of sickness. Because shamanism is also performance art, the best shamans were, and still are, poets and actors, able to dramatize with costume, gesture, and word their otherworldly adventures. Traditionally, like their cousins in Native America, shamans were distinguished by special clothing, protective amulets, and other symbolic imagery. These items served to mark their extraordinary social status.

One of the shamans' most idiosyncratic gifts is his or her ability to travel through this stratified universe. The shaman can transcend the limitations of the human condition by passing safely through monstrous obstacles barring the way to the other world. This ecstatic trance or altered state of consciousness is central to the art of shamanism. The shamanic trance is an out-of-body experience during which the shaman feels him or herself to be in communication with the spirit world. To trigger the ecstatic state, the shaman may employ one or more of the 200 species of hallucinogenic plants, including species of cacti and mushrooms. Not all shamans used hallucinogenic substances, though. On the Great Plains, non-chemical techniques of ecstasy were sometimes used, such as sensory deprivation, hunger, self-torture, sleeplessness, lonely vigil, exposure to the elements, meditation, yoga-like positions, song, dance, drumming, and so on. The shaman's ability to endure such dramatic hyperstimulation or hypoattenuation of our sensory system is truly formidable.

When shamans enter non-ordinary states of shamanic awareness, they are thrust beyond our conditioned, three-dimensional view of reality and into a realm where they can gain relevant insights about the unseen world. This is accompanied by a profound sense of interconnectedness and reverence for all life. The deeply transformational state of wholeness inherent in transcending the collective hypnotic slumber of humans serves to awaken their spiritual "vision."

Shamanism recognizes and works with the core human yearning for a life in harmony with the universe and the intertwining of material and spiritual worlds. As more heed the call of healing service to our planet, the path of universal shamanism is being embraced as a human evolutionary imperative.

Contemporary shamans expand the ancestral paths of psychic awareness and spiritual wisdom to the problems of our planet. They understand that Gaia or *Pachamama*—Quechua for Mother Earth—is a conscious, living being, and that all of life is interconnected in delicate and dynamic balance. They know how to awaken and tap into their psychic gifts to cultivate spiritual discernment through the development of inner vision. By aligning with the forces of nature, great healing power becomes available to them as interdependent luminous strands in loving service to the Great Web of Life. The shaman serves to remind us of the natural human ability to tap into innate psychic and spiritual essence, so we can consciously transform our lives.

Through an internal dialogue between ourselves and the environment, we create an opening with which to connect to the power, wisdom, and love—*kallpa*, *yachay*, and *munay*, respectively—within all things. The dialogue is not only in words but in symbols and images that spring from a place within us that senses a more holographic, interdependent experience of ourselves in relationship to the universe around us. Universal Shamanism embodies a time-honored living cosmovision, a soul-animated and spiritually infused worldview that offers the practitioner an experiential link between the architecture of the universe and the patterns of nature. It integrates these notions and forges a system of interdependent relationships between the cosmic and the Divine with human society and individual destiny.

Ideas about the structure of the world, about the rhythms of time, and about the origin of the cosmos are all woven into a sacred, ceremonial landscape expressed though our progressive ritual mastery of shamanic healing arts. For those walking this "good medicine" path, the sacred is not a theoretical idea, but an experience of being deeply connected with everything in the visible universe and all the unseen forces that lie behind it. When we experience this evolutionary sense of universal belonging—through which humanity is bonded in shared reverence of the heavens above and the Earth below—life becomes engaging and meaningful, an embodiment of the starlight from which all things flow.

In essence, any heartfelt creation of a shamanic healing setting is equivalent to a ceremonially consecrated imaginal map of the universe or archetypal cosmic landscape, which "energetically" anchors both seen and unseen dimensions of the *Anima Mund*i (i.e., World Soul) before the shamanic practitioner. It is a beautiful container of Spirit, and it is also a soul-infused artifact of the material world. It is a living, dynamic pattern upon which and within which we can consciously do our evolutionary personal and planetary healing work.

Initiates into Universal Shamanism ceremonial practice embrace their ancestral lineage, not because it is superior to all other traditions, but because its effects are healthfully liberating and aesthetically graceful. It is a visually dramatic and sensually rich ritual art, which appeals to those who resonate with the healing power in natural patterns, Earth rhythms, and cosmic cycles. It is also a *syncretistic* shamanic tradition, which means it is openly tolerant and widely inclusive of diverse cultural ideologies, religious beliefs, and all world wisdom traditions. Hence, your Universal Shamanism ritual setting is discerningly designed to become a pristine reflection of the individual practitioner's ontological sense of sacred belonging and evolutionary purpose within the Great Cosmic Web of Life.

WALKING IN BEAUTY

A simple observation of the natural world reveals that change is the only constant in life. Transformation is an inherent aspect of our experience within the Great Originating Mystery we call Creation. Within all expressions of the phenomenal world that we witness, rarely do we see any stagnation, any stoppage. Instead, it is all flux, it is all flow. Creation is all a fluid process of refining and deepening our consciousness as immortal souls. Being aligned with the understanding that change and transformation are unifying evolutionary principles behind all expressions of life, seen and unseen, is the natural way to walk in balance, equilibrium, and reverence upon this good Earth, while ever expanding our awareness of interdependence and our inextricable unity with the Great Sacred Web of Life. That is the importance of transformation. As we raise that awareness globally, we return to a beauty walk on this good planet, *Pachamama*.

To reclaim the inherent wholeness that is our human birthright, we must first reclaim our co-creative power to birth and sustain heartfelt, sacred community—to openly embrace our participation and our belonging as a planetary family. Universal Shamanism as an Earth-honoring, healing path can help us to do that. This path provides the tools necessary for us to walk a path of deep dialogue and deep listening with each other, with our living Earth, and with Great Spirit.

Part One

The unique compilation of stories that follows concerns shamanic healing and spiritual awakening born of each author's self-transformational encounter with non-ordinary reality. The collection is a veritable gift of beauty and soul-awakening wisdom of great service to those new to shamanic studies, as well as to experienced practitioners of these sacred arts.

PART TWO

Personal Quests of Communion with Nature and Creation

Tongues in trees, books in running brooks, sermons in stones, and good in everything.

—WILLIAM SHAKESPEARE

FROM ASTHMA TO APOTHEOSIS

My coming back into wholeness as a soul on this good Earth began at first breath. Inspiration, and Spirit itself, filled my lungs as life took hold. My Peruvian physician father looked lovingly upon me as I breathed. My Italian American mother relaxed.

Yet, what began so easily became a struggle for survival as I grew. As asthma set in, my breath was simply not available. I felt distant from Spirit and distant from life itself at those times. I was a young soul encased within a physical body. As a seed that had not yet sprouted, my soul lay dormant, deep underground. Rather than expansion and growth, my soul befriended contraction to survive. Rather than movement, it welcomed stillness. Rather than the radiant sunlight of day, it came to anticipate the darkness of an artificial harbor.

In my first nine years, I had learned many ways to appear sane as my family descended ever further into dysfunction. Violence and danger had become the norm. Amid all the chaos, my breathing became more and more constricted. Sometimes, I held my breath for fear I would be heard and simply add to the chaos and the stress. My asthma attacks became more frequent. I began to withdraw. I missed day after day of school as I struggled just to breathe. Meanwhile, I found refuge in small spaces, under tables and in corners. I crawled in the classroom as perplexed children pointed fingers, laughing, and mocking me. I was like a scared animal, hiding.

When I was ten years old, and the finest physicians in Lima agreed that my survival depended on leaving our coastal city and moving to the dry central highlands. I felt a stirring as we rode up the winding roads, away from sea-level Lima and into the central Andes. As we traveled, we followed the *Rimac* River, named by the Quechua-speaking peoples of the highlands because *rimac* means "the one who speaks." My destiny was calling out to me, and I could feel the murmuring voices of my ancestors tumble down the mountainsides into its flow.

Our destination was the town of Chosica, halfway between the coast and the highest peaks of the Andes. There, giant stones and enigmatic citadels loom high above the village. They are venerated today, just as they were during ancestral times. The entire region is known as a place of visitation, sightings, and actual contact with star-beings. My father chose Chosica hoping that the drier, cleaner air might help my hypoxia. It was there where I found breath, through an encounter with the beyond.

It was a December night in 1961. The air was cold and the sky full of stars. My mother had put me to bed and then returned to the kitchen to clean up after dinner. From deepest slumber, I awoke with a start. My eyes were wide and round in surprise and growing desperation. My mouth was just a slit, and I felt my chest disappearing. My body felt completely numb. There was no breath at all. I tried desperately to call for help, yet I could not move or speak. The world began closing in on me as darkness pressed down against my chest. The Earth opened to swallow me. I felt myself pulled down through the mattress of my bed, deeper and deeper into this abyss. I felt cold. The pounding in my ears that was my heart became faint, then fainter still. And then all was silent. I relaxed and let myself drown in the sensation of peace.

I was dead.

From far away, I began hearing someone call my name. It wasn't my birth name, but a nickname my father had given me years before because of my curiosity and my countenance. "Eager Beaver," he had called me—"Beaver" for short. It felt good to have an animal name, and I identified with it. Faintly, I began hearing it in my right ear, then in my left, "Beaver, Beaver, come back. We need you. Beaver, come back, Beeeeaver…"

Suddenly, with a gasp of air, I was pulled from the abyss that had swallowed me. I found myself sitting upright in my bed in total darkness.

I gazed around the room as I regained consciousness more fully. Then I began to feel the presence of extraordinary compassion, love, healing, and grace. As I gazed deeper into the darkness, there appeared a quivering field of luminosity that gradually settled into three, humanlike forms. Standing seven feet tall, their heads were almost touching the low ceiling of my room. They became increasingly more detailed and separate, their appearance more discernable.

All three had long white beards and luminous blue eyes. They were ancient, yet ageless; wizened, yet completely unencumbered. They wore long white robes, and their long hair grew into wispy trails of luminous, spiraling light. They were three angelic beings, three Shining Ones. I now know them to be the three expressions of the Divine that have been described in tales and legends since the dawn of time: luminous beings, perfect, harmonious, whole. They were beyond all dichotomy and division. They were Absolute Love.

These three beings communicated in unison a thought that mirrored exactly what I felt. A resounding gift of awakening to my true place of origin reverberated deep within me. The thought-feeling coursed from my head through the length of my body. It felt pleasant, like the vibrational lingering of sacred words. In that moment, my entire experience of being in a physical body shifted. I recognized my own essence in the light that they embodied.

Part Two

That awareness alone would have been enough for me to embrace the experience of death that had come upon me. In that instant, I could have just let go, returning with a peaceful heart to the hands of our Maker. Yet somehow, I knew it was not my time.

The moment I recognized this, the radiant one to my left bent his tall frame toward me and placed his transparent lips to my chest. For what seemed an eternity, he sucked in though his lips, extracting from my frail body all residue of the illness that had hindered the evolution of my soul in this lifetime. Afterward, he raised his head and offered that density in breath up to the heavens. I saw the crack between the worlds in that moment. All my suffering, guilt, and misconceptions were taken skyward as he blew into the heavens. When he finished, the portal vanished as quickly as it had appeared.

Next, the shining one to my right placed his right hand—with a luminous, open-fingered palm—upon my sternum. He placed his left palm on top of the right one. As he closed his deep blue eyes, I felt a concentrated willing: a bestowal of his essence into my heart. My entire being was lit from within as I lay motionless on the bed.

Meanwhile, the being who stood between the other two opened his eyes wide, looking straight ahead. His Buddha-like hands danced with flowing light. He touched his luminous fingertips together in various gestures and then rested his arms by his side and gazed toward me. His eyes held infinite compassion. It was then that the communication between us began.

I entered a realm between dream and waking where images floated seamlessly along. The first image I was gifted by that luminous being was of returning to Lima. I saw the great turmoil that would ensue as my father and mother separated, yet I saw myself being free of asthma forever. I saw myself being able to run and jump and ride a bicycle as well as swim in the ocean and play in the school yard. I saw myself with my classmates, having crushes and experiencing the fullness of that very sensitive age between late childhood and young adulthood.

This telepathic transmission of the events of my life was extensive. I saw the jobs I would hold, the relationships I would treasure, the children who would be born, and the people who would be lost to me in the dance of eros that accompanies the search for self. I saw the teachers I would meet, and I witnessed the artistry of what I was born to do as my service to the Great Web of Life.

As the movie of my life began to fade from view, the last message reverberating through my soul was this: "Remember the rituals. Remember the rituals. Remember the rituals."

For the next several years, my recollection of that transformational moment was clouded. That changed in August of 1969 when I met the famed *huachumero*, don Celso Rojas Palomino from Salas, Chiclayo. It happened during what was to be the first of many *sanpedrito* ceremonies.

That first night, after the tobacco offering was given and after his patients were cleansed with the sacred objects on his altar, out of the center of his *banco*, a light started to circulate. I blinked my eyes in amazement. The light continued to rise from the mesa and, as it emerged, it coalesced into a large, oval, pulsing field. Before my eyes, the same three wizened Shining Ones that had healed me of asthma eight years earlier appeared. I stared in open-mouthed wonder. No one else seemed to see them—not even don Celso's assistants, who were sitting just to his left.

Was I dreaming? Was this really happening?

At first, I didn't notice don Celso's sideways glance. Then he elbowed me firmly, jarring me from my reverie and asking, "Do you remember them?"

"Yes, I do," I stuttered.

At that moment, my entire reality shifted. I felt transported back in time to a moment I had all but forgotten. In less than a nanosecond, everything that had been shown to me at age ten during that near-death experience came back into my awareness. I remembered everything. In this second visitation

Part Two

by the three Shining Ones, I was able to tap into the noosphere—the ineffable yet universal field of information that some call the Akashic record.

In that moment, all contrasts, all polarities, all separation, all interpretation, all need to have a nice, comforting, orderly world was annihilated. It was all destroyed. I found myself floating up into space and dissolving as a separate entity, as an individual, as an ego-mind, as a personality. In that moment, the one known to this world by the name Oscar just disappeared. I was *absorbed* within the *All*.

I remembered my purpose for being born, and this time, it stayed firmly imprinted in my psyche. All that I had witnessed and forgotten at age ten came cascading back, free of censorship and dimensional filters. I realized how incomplete our sensory experiences are as I peeked behind the veil of the eternal *now*.

As soon as the ritual ended, I asked don Celso if I might apprentice with him, and he agreed.

Viewed from the perspective of a heartfelt shamanic initiation, I now understand the true miracle of love that was at the root of my illness. The severe asthma that had been part of my life for so long had been the very path to my redemption. It pointed the way for my return to wholeness. It had paved the road from the dark night of my aching soul to the superior realms of my shamanic ancestors.

Oscar Miro-Quesada

A RIVER HAPPENING

For as long as I can remember, I have been a lucid dreamer and a nightmare purveyor. From the earliest age, I've tiptoed carefully into the night, joining with deities and the dead to walk dark worlds and see the unseen.

One night several years ago, I woke up not knowing where I was, or who I was. As I came to, I could not recall my name, where I was living, or anything else. It took several seconds to gather these pieces. My boyfriend of that time was standing by the window, looking at me in a different way than ever before.

I acted as if I just had the most refreshing night's sleep, as though everything was normal, but he seemed unnerved. Small talk wasn't shaking the shock from him, so I simply addressed it.

"I don't know where I went," I said.

He gave me a sideways glance. "You were gone. Gone," he said. "You went somewhere. You left."

He was right. I had left but I didn't know why, or where I'd traveled to. I was used to it. From my earliest days, sleeping and awake had always been fluid, like two sides of the same coin.

Part Two

Western New York, where I was born, is known for its bizarre and severe weather. There was something about the animate weather and my lucid dreaming that seemed to give me deeper sight into the elements, land, and spirit world. These forces were alive with conversation, and with stories, often involving indigenous peoples present even before white settlers came.

As a Caucasian girl raised in a Roman Catholic family, I didn't know much about indigenous peoples for my first four years. But standing on the edge of an ancient ravine one afternoon with my father, I would learn.

He held my hand as I took in the presence of tree adults, land elders, river siblings, and Mother Sun all around us. I listened to these elemental forces of my nature family conversing energetically about something that was coming toward us. Wary, I inched in closer to my dad and looked up for reassurance. He had a serene smile on his face like he was receiving the beauty of Mother Nature. Feeling better, I looked through the spaces between the tree trunks in front of us, waiting to see what was coming.

In the distance, I heard voices of Indigenous men coming down the river. They were intoning a low, rhythmic chant that caused my tree relatives to bend and wave wildly in the wind. It was as if the men arriving had stirred something; either alarm, reverence, or both.

The elemental forces whipped and bent things more dramatically. Somewhat frightened, I drew in closer to my father. My tiny, outstretched arm began to tingle from my dad holding it up for so long, but I kept my eyes fixed on the spaces between the trees as the harmonic chanting got closer and the tip of a canoe came into view.

More of the canoe appeared until I could see all of it and six larger-than-life, Indigenous men in full brightly colored headdresses. The air was scented from their leathery, worn clothes. In awe, I watched as they glided into view, three facing the center on either side.

Bracing myself because the luring chants pulled me into a different state, I found it hard to look away. My tree relatives began groaning under the force of gravity, to which they seemed to relinquish control.

Pressing closer to my father's leg, feeling the warmth of his jeans on my cold cheek, I continued to peek out from beneath my eyelids. One of the men looked at me with intention, as if the boat had slowed to traverse with me just for this moment.

I looked back at his gaping eyes and although his expression was unreadable, his movements toward me were like that of a crouching animal waiting to pounce. His intense gaze locked into mine, and in an instant, he leaped ... into me.

With no way to understand this, I looked up at my dad, whose face held the same expression as if nothing had passed. The canoe drifted down the river and out of view.

My mother's voice called out from a distance. "Come on you two," she motioned toward her.

When we reached the car, I slid in along the long vinyl seat in front to be between the safety of my mom and dad. I could see my nature relatives returning slowly to the present moment and was reassured by the familiar bickering and tussling sounds of my sisters in the back seat.

As we pulled out of the gravel-strewn parking lot, I began talking about "the Indians in the canoe" with the same kind of dramatic mannerisms as my nature family just a few moments before. My dad stopped the car to look over at my mother with a confused glance. He was shaking his head, 'no.'

"She sounds so sure," my mother said to him, "Was there a historical reenactment or something?"

My dad continued to shake his head. I continued to describe what I'd seen in detail without mentioning what had happened. A part of me was hoping they'd seen the Indigenous men on the river too.

Part Two

"There were no Indians on the river," they shared, looking at one another for backup.

"Sometimes our minds play tricks on us," my dad said.

"It means you have a vivid imagination," my mother added.

Even as a five-year-old, I knew this was beyond their scope of understanding. I felt a strong urge to protect them too and to keep what I'd experienced to myself. On the way home, I remained attentive and sweet, but inside I was grappling with deep philosophical and theological questions that I had no vocabulary yet to unpack.

A key question was whether I was still part of my own family, or now part of this indigenous tribe. Did he jump *into* me in that momentary encounter, or was I taken into them?

For days afterward, I tried to see if anything about me had changed. I noticed I felt grateful and an awareness of a deeply intimate space within me—almost like a distant and sacred land—that gave me access to a different kind of knowing, to an ancient, indigenous way of perceiving and being in the world.

Over time, I would become what some may call "a seer" who experiences lucid dreams each night, premonitions, visitations, and more. And at times, I'd have precious shamanic experiences that would "happen upon me." These allowed me to time travel and world walk, often creating great healing and catharsis from issues in my past or present life.

These shamanic encounters led me to challenge societal beliefs about dominating Mother Earth, exploitation, scientific rationalism, three-dimensional space and time, linear thinking, patriarchal hierarchies, and other ideas.

The happening on the river facilitated a journey to awareness, deepening my relationship to self, others, and the natural world. It was foundational for developing another perspective, and for my unique relationship to Spirit, which has served me and blessed me.

Allison Kenny

CLAIMING POWER FROM OUR PAST

"So, what do you think the bear wants, David?" These were the words asked by a Pachakuti Mesa Tradition practitioner and guide some 15 years ago.

A terrible and life-threatening burn during childhood had left me imprisoned behind a fortress of scarred walls and armored identity. Focusing on the illusion of control and on repressing empathetic receptivity caused my isolating rage to continue to burn. I remained stalked by anxiety, depression, and anger as a young adult and parent. I likened this ever-present emotional beast to an enormous grizzly bear, ready to strike me down and consume me.

For much of my adult life, this was my existence, being chased down with the sound of massive paws hitting the ground behind me, holding nothing but anger as protection. The one place that this "bear" that stalked me left me at peace was in the ancient mountains of North Georgia, which bears call home.

But then, the medicine came. With great care and ritual artistry, the practitioner led me on a shamanic journey to the shadow world within, to the *ukhupacha*. As the slow, pulsing drum strikes deepened my inner gaze and ushered me into an ancient and evocative world, I soon felt that great bear's

Part Two

presence behind me. The bear was so close, I could hear it draw a breath, yet I was strangely calm. It was exhaustion that overwhelmed me, not fear. Drained from a lifetime of being stalked and a constant sense of impending carnage, I simply surrendered to the chase in the journey.

Stopping and turning, I faced the beast, asking, "What do you want with me?"

Fully expecting to be ripped to pieces and devoured, I was utterly amazed by the bear's answer.

I am your protector. I am your power, Bear said, a kind look in his eyes.

Anxiety and rage melted as my vista immediately expanded in beholding the truth. Yielding to the love present, I allowed him to strip me of the steel-clad aspects of self that no longer served me, and that had leached into and diseased the waters of my relationships. My own relationship to my past was instantly changed.

While preoccupied with a delusional sense of disconnection, I had mistaken the healing bear of protection as being a threat. I began to reawaken to the truth that I was a necessary part of the universe. This world needed me—and those like me, the wounded ones. It needs all our brokenness and pain. In truth, the world needs us because of our brokenness and pain.

Recognizing that we are an integral part of something bigger than ourselves makes us both a giver and receiver. It is within our power to contribute that for which the world longs: empathy that makes way for loving, compassionate, spiritually attuned connection, with "All Our Relations."

David Jordan

SOUL TO SOUL SIBLINGS

"*Your* dad never went to see her," my mom gently explained. Sitting around the sun infused kitchen nook gazing out at the billowing clouds overlooking the lake, my mom continued, "He would drive me to the children's home and wait outside while I went in. Dad couldn't do it, and he never saw her again after she was born."

Nearly fifty years had gone by before I'd heard this story. My only living sibling and I were visiting our parents, and I was querying our mom and grandmother about family history.

They rarely talked about Lori Ann much, my younger sister who never came home from the hospital yet lived to be nearly two years old. This was a rare occasion they were open to talking about her and that time.

In 1972 when I was nearly seven years old, Mom became pregnant again. My parents, who had always wanted many children, had difficulty conceiving for many years. Now I was going to get a younger brother or sister. Excitement filled the wider family.

I have few memories of this time, but I remember my pregnant mom at the kitchen sink washing dishes. I picture a new baby's room lovingly prepared to welcome this much wanted second child. When the time came,

Part Two

I can imagine my parents rushed to the hospital while my grandparents watched me, and we all waited with anticipation for my parents to bring the newborn home. But she never came home.

It's now 2020, and I'm at an ayahuasca retreat, sitting outside on a warm spring day with my journal and musing on my intention for the night's ceremony. For the last two years working with this beautiful master teacher plant, I'd always focused on my own healing needs; yet for this retreat, my desire is to bring healing for my female living relatives: my mom and sister.

Lying on the freshly mown grass, I muse about ancestral traumas and patterns and how illness and diseases pass generationally. Mom and Sis were having strange life parallels. Both have thyroid issues, and both were pregnant at a time when another family member died.

The medication Mom started taking in the '70s was later determined to cause birth defects. At the time, it was deemed safe, but Lori Ann was born with multiple issues and could not come home to live with us; instead, she was placed in a children's home about a half hour's drive away. I was never allowed to meet her, and only my mother and grandmother made the journey to visit her. Now decades later, my sister is awaiting surgery to remove tumors near her thyroid.

Later that evening at the retreat's temple space, we prepare for the healing plant ceremony. One by one, we are called to drink the medicinal, earthy-tasting elixir.

My intention tonight, Madre Ayahuasca, is to be a vessel for healing for my family. Please help heal the trauma my mother carries about her second daughter, Lori Ann. Please help me release anything that does not serve our family. Please help break any patterns so that my nieces do not carry this forward.

Sitting in complete darkness, I silently repeat my intention while awaiting the plant's effects. My belly gurgles as the medicine is absorbed. Although I repeat mantras to keep my mind focused, I slowly become unable to hold onto the words. My mind drifts.

What was it like for my parents to leave for the hospital and then come home without a baby? How did my mother possibly contain her grief? Who was available to take care of her?

And what about me, little me? What did I feel when no baby came home? Who was there to take care of me? How did I ever make sense of this?

Whoosh. I slide deeper into the kaleidoscopic universe of the medicine, and I am transported back to my seven-year-old self. I feel the excitement of waiting for a baby sibling to come home as buoyant jubilation courses through my physical body. And then a flood of sadness erupts when it doesn't happen. Tears stream down my cheeks as I weep for little me.

Where did I go?

Grandma, Grandpa, and all my aunties and uncles appear. Warmth infuses my whole being as I tap into their vast love received during childhood. Suddenly, Lori Ann materializes in energetic form. We meet for the first time—child to child, soul to soul.

Are you okay? Why? Why did it have to happen this way? I ask.

It was my soul's contract. It is what was chosen. Everything is perfect. Let me show you, she responds.

Our energies mingle and our souls dance together in play for many hours. Sobs of bliss and grief intertwine as she teaches my seven-year-old self about compassion. My adult body nestles into the wall behind me, and I curl up with a blanket while my mind continues to travel the multiverse.

Lori Ann tells me she's always been with us, watching from a different realm. Simultaneous feelings of grief, bliss, empathy, and love expand my heart as we embrace. I am overjoyed to be with her. After several hours of communing together, my younger self comes to a peaceful understanding of her short time on earth.

Part Two

Months after that ceremony, I realized I had a soul retrieval; I brought back a part of my younger self cast off during the trauma of my sister's absence and wove little me back into my earthly adult body.

While the ayahuasca journey didn't bring direct healing to my living family members, I know that my encounter with Lori Ann will positively affect the wider family field and future generations. Most of all, I will never forget meeting my younger sister heart to heart, soul to soul.

Kathy Guidi

SIWA AND THE AMAZIGH WOMEN

On an exhausting seven-hour journey through the dry, hot desert of Egypt, I receive a message from a powerful tribe of ancient times—the Amazigh people. In my vision, I see and sense a Bedouin man from another timeline riding a camel alongside our car. His face is covered by a dark blue turban, and his eyes glow like intense, mystical coals. He is the messenger of the Heart of Siwa, the guardian of this oasis at the heart of the desert and seeks to inform her if I will respect the hidden wisdom stored in ancient timelines.

As he rides away in my vision, I feel myself being watched. A beautiful, dark-skinned woman appears before my inner eye and presents herself as Siwa's guardian. She welcomes me to enter her oasis, which contains a once beautiful temple surrounded by lush palm trees, flowers, and a crystal-clear spring. I feel deeply connected to this Bedouin guardian, who once was a priestess of the oracle temple in what is now called Siwa; she may have even been an oracle for Alexander the Great.

She speaks these words of wisdom to me.

It is important to connect with ancient places of power and the web of the universe that weaves through everything natural. It is important to disconnect

Part Two

from old patterns and programs that connect us to the artificial system. We can trust. Natural places send signals that call us. The true culmination is to vibrate in harmony with the universe, nature, and the highest natural frequency. It means tuning into the infinite vibrational field of the universe and resonating with all that is natural and sacred.

The desert is the sacred fire, the fire of the heart that can warm but also burn. In the past, women took sand to see where the wind came from and where there was water. The fire and the desert need the water. Where heat and water come together, steam is created, and the rainbow formed.

When we unite extreme polarities within us, the bridge for something new is created. When the fire has burned away everything in us that is not natural, we will pass through the void and let go of everything unnatural to return home, to the natural cycles of life.

The void is the source where we let go of everything. We lose ourselves and surrender completely to trust the Divine. Then the gate will open to the heart of the desert, the source of your heart in which everything is created.

With a sudden inhale, I return from this vision and thank the guardian. As we arrive at the Siwa Oasis, I realize I have a mission to accomplish.

We travel early the next day to the oracle temple and arrive as the first sunrays are kissing the ancient site awake. There are several myths about this temple's founding. One tells of two dark-skinned priestesses from the temple of Amun in Thebes (modern Luxor) who were banished to the desert. In this legend, one founded the temple of Dodona in Greece, becoming the voice of the oracle there. The second priestess, after a time in Libya, came to Siwa to eventually serve as the sibyl of the oracle.

A snake greets us at the entrance to the temple, and a white dove flies over the site. The contradictory signs confirm that there is something to complete here.

A walk of the streets of Siwa Oasis on my last day reveals mostly men on the street, as women here are not allowed to buy food in the market. All married women must wear a burqa, a one-piece garment with a black veil that covers the face and body; they must wear it even when temperatures climb above 104 degrees Fahrenheit. Married women are not allowed to be seen by other men after marriage; most importantly, these women must cover their eyes.

The village's energy feels completely unbalanced from the Divine Feminine. Shocked by how much this touches me, I also intuitively know that the energy imbalance is being revealed for a reason. This place screams to me in its silence, of women who are unheard underneath their burqas, and birds who sing an old forgotten song about freedom.

The previous sighting of the snake at the temple had signaled that there is still poison in this place, which wants to finally shed its old skin. The dove was a harbinger of peace and purity.

With these signs from the intelligent web of life now understood, I humbly ask permission that afternoon to enter the holy place.

Only dusty ruins await me at the oracle temple. Wandering around as if lost, it feels as if oblivion has veiled all, and the wind whispers through a hollow bone. Numb and confused by this, I realize that this feeling is coming from the feminine collective. I gather my clarity and seek out the most powerful place there: the sanctuary of the oracle temple.

Sitting down, I open my *mesa*, or medicine bundle, of 13 stones and crystals that have been energetically connected to an ancient lineage of earthkeepers called the *Pampamesayok* from Peru. I take my sistrum, an ancient Egyptian rattle, in one hand, and staff with the head of Horus in the other and begin to rattle.

Humbly, I ask for my spiritual guides' support, and for healing of this place for the highest good of all. I call upon *munay*, the cosmic unconditional energy field of love, to fill this place. Through my sistrum comes a clinking sound that chases away old patriarchal energies. The staff of Horus channels light, effervescent energy from Source into the temple; pure *Sami*.

Part Two

Tremendous energy and light suddenly flow through me and down into the earth of this place to purify various ley lines and timelines. My inner vision brings the sight of ancient Amazigh women, priestesses, healers, and wisdom keepers coming from different directions, dimensions, realities, and worlds, and approaching the oracle temple energetically.

Joining them while all timelines are open are *Paqarinas,* female *Pampamesayoks,* and wisdom keepers, walking through time and space to enter the temple in joy and happiness. They throw their hats in the air, laugh, and say, *Finally we are back.*

It is as if hundreds had physically reassembled in the temple of bliss to reunite and to be equal on all levels of life. They turn to me and thank me, and I am deeply touched and cry. The intense energy present makes me tremble.

In part, this is from receiving a powerful stream of consciousness through me, which shares that women of this time will come back here, too, and remember. They will remember their seer and oracle powers to create beauty, heal wounds, reunite, heal our collective broken souls, and allow the lost to come home. It is a vision of the return of the Divine Feminine to all aspects of life. These women will travel to this place and remember that they were part of the great oracle, the Great Mystery.

After a time, the strong energies calm down and peace fills me and the site. Opening my eyes, I realize this is just another step into the mystery of the great Divine intelligence. With gratitude, I leave this sacred site, knowing now that many lightworkers are connected here and working for the highest good of all.

Heading out on the departure day to our car that will take us to Cairo to start the journey home, my gaze brushes on a picture I missed before that hangs in the hotel's reception area. Stepping closer to this painting, I am stunned to find myself beholding the eyes of the woman seen in my journey to the desert.

"Who is that?" I ask the man at the counter and learn that she was one of the female Amazigh who guarded the temple and served as oracles here long ago.

Looking into her eyes, she smiles at me through time and space. I smile back.

Annette Assmy

THE BONES OF MY HEART

Burnished with a coppery brown patina from age, the bone glows against the white sand where it rests over 20 feet from the lake's scalloped wave lines. No footprints of people or animals surround it, and the sand tightly envelopes the edges of its femur shape. Driftwood dragons are common here, but fossilized bones are a rare find. I have the intriguing sensation of someone handing it to me as I reach for it and wonder of its connection to the previous night's ceremony.

My youth had been spent exploring a moss- and fern-covered mountain, vying with bears for blueberries, and sifting sand for arrowheads on another remote lake shore. This lively lake has become a regular place of solace for its familiar sounds of crashing waves, wind swishing through pine branches, and hidden forest creatures' talk. I deeply desire that my child, who comes here with me, will also learn to treasure such wild places. I watch her visibly expand when we arrive here–arms catching the wind, bare feet churning up the sand. We dig and build things between forays into the frigid surf, replenishing our aliveness.

Stashed among my camping gear is a bin of art objects that I have been intuitively collecting in recent years. Each embodies and embraces a fragment

Part Two

of an inexorable, mystical healing journey. As a steady, colorful succession of shamans and healers have been sharing their eclectic wisdom with me, a remembrance of something–a deeply held something–of unnamable importance gets recorded in the art.

Much of this artistic, magical part of my life I have hidden from others; but something inside me is shifting, and I am drawn to honor the mysterious muse with a ceremony in an expansive wild setting.

So, the previous evening, after a campfire feast, my friend and my daughter frolicked on the waterfront while I rolled heavy, colorful beach boulders into a huge circle. A fierce dragonhead stone anchored the center. As dusk descended, candles glowed in jars, and the fragrant medicine of sage, tobacco, and lavender formed a protective sensory field. Rattle, necklace, wand, and staff; all joined my "holy" stone collection on the altar.

I shook out my black silk medicine wheel skirt. Adorned with glinting gemstones hung on a spiderweb of colored threads, it had been created under the supervision of a porch raven over several days in a remote cabin as an act of power. The seashells around the hem of the skirt tinkled as I donned my brightly colored, tasseled "hummingbird" shawl and picked up my handmade elk drum.

While the waters stilled and the night sky filled with a weighty darkness, I called the directions, elements, and helpers to inhabit their seats in the ceremony. My two companions snuggled into blankets nearby, and I soon forgot about them as the invoked energy pulled me into the celebration.

Shuffle-dancing the perimeter of the stone mandala, I drummed, sang, and offered my handmade creations to the service of the Great Mystery.

"Hey, hey, heya, hey." The prayer song rose strong and free from somewhere deep within. "Hoom, humma, hey."

Filled suddenly with great purpose, my calls became a cosmic wail, wrenching centuries-old pain from my body. Every breath dredged up more to be released in the sounds that escaped me. Time disappeared as the unnamable energy of the darkness drank of the offering. The song gradually calmed, the circle came back into visual focus, and the energies were thanked.

After stowing my treasures at the campsite, I joined my companions at the beach, where night creatures prowled the darkness. The air was crisp and clear, and our senses keen. We tucked into sleeping bags, leaning back on an enormous driftwood tree trunk, and watched stars streaming and sparkling on the ultimate big screen. The dark lake brought their reflections right up to the shoreline, and we sat, mesmerized, on the edge of the world.

The next morning, I exit our ancient orange and brown hippy camper into a dappled dawn, a wonderful spaciousness in my being, and deep gratitude for life. It had been my first experience calling Spirit to flow through me in an offering ceremony; and the world feels fresh.

We hike before breakfast along the beach, looking for animal tracks and stirring up seagulls and eagles from their morning conference. It is on the way back that my eyes have fallen upon the massive leg bone. *How did I miss it before?* Holding it for a long time, I wonder where it is from, how it got here, and why it had shown up in this moment. I feel it is a gift and a greeting card—an acknowledgment of my heartfelt, innocent shamanic offering of energy the previous night.

Others seem to file my bone story under the interesting-but-not-that-exciting category. So, I keep the delight mostly to myself savoring what would become one of several anchor points for my life.

Another ceremony to call in healing occurs eight years later at the same lake. A divorce, several exhausting moves, the relationship with my daughter now in tatters, I return to the wild shoreline. This time, my new partner happily wanders about from a distance, keeping a watch out for cougars and bears.

"Hey, hey, hooma, hey." Like a spell being broken, the soul song twists and extracts the painful energy held in my spine.

"Hoom, humma, hey." I expand to feel 14 feet tall as an immense loving energy fills the void.

When we wander back from the sacred circle the following dawn, I feel clear and bright, with a sense of hopefulness and acceptance. While sharing the old story of finding a bone after such a ceremony, I come across a smaller one, sitting in the open near where I'd found the first one years before. This bronze, fist-shaped fragment shares the identical color and patina.

For me it seems an act of compassionate caring, delivered in a customized language, and in a tangible form to hold in reverence. The universe begins to feel less random, and this place, a possible stable portal of connection, feels like a supportive, spiritual home base.

My cousin comes with me a year later to share a vacation during a busy lake season. My treasured beach is narrow and weedy from high water levels and the campers are crowded together. We walk further away to a wildish spot to undertake the childlike creation of a circle on the shoreline; this time inhabited by quirky, stacked-stone people wearing tiny hats and seaweed hair. We joyfully beachcomb and create art under a pop-up gazebo at the campsite.

The mood changes one afternoon after learning that my father's dear friend has taken his own life. I am moved to hold a healing ceremony that evening, and my cousin chooses to sit quietly nearby. With Spirit's support and songs soaring once again, I bless the one who has walked-on for his journey and send comfort to those left behind. The transition's heavy energy rocks my body yet clears to a peaceful knowing that all is well with him.

Hiking out the next morning to see how our little stone friends have fared overnight, we find that other campers have coated the entire circle in black and white sand, creating a huge yin/yang pattern. In our laughter during that expansive moment, I tell my cousin of the strange occurrence finding the two magic bones recalling, "I found them somewhere around…here." In that moment, inconceivably, at my feet I see a third bone.

Undeniably, the spirits of this land have heard my sacred calls. I am beginning to see my shamanic journey as a giant, spiritual scavenger hunt that has me traveling, seeking, experimenting, listening, feeling, noticing, and deciding. Slivers of sacred light are reaching through the crust of my earthly experience, allowing a glimpse into much more through two-way conversations with a mysterious force that welcomes me, cares for me, and is part of me. Finding timely messages, treasures, teachers, and friends no longer count as "coincidences." These daily events are creating a comfort zone for spiritual interaction.

The three bones of my heart now lie in the shape of a pelvis, surrounding and supporting the shell at the center of my Pachakuti Mesa Tradition altar. The bones' presence steadies my earth walk by providing benevolent, loving, and nourishing energies that "re-member" me and remind me that the presence of other people is a vital part of the journey.

During deep new moon nights, the bones often draw me from my bed into conversation at the candlelit altar, reorienting me to the wild lunar cycle of Gaia. A smile and expansive sense of heart comes then, in considering the possibility that the one who reaches across the mystic bridge of ceremony and gives these magical anchors to me is, in fact, myself.

Adele Goodwin Keleher

MY SHAMANIC HEALING

The sun fades slowly over the mountains in Oregon as I walk down towards our yurt by the cool, clear waters of the Breitenbush River.

The fir and cedar trees form archways above like cathedral vaults, shrouding me in the sacred. There is no division here between the inner and the outer. Kindness, respect, and reciprocity to each other, the land, and Nature infuses everything.

Hank Wesselman, our shamanic guide, is going to lead a healing ceremony for someone with an illness who wishes to be healed. Like everyone else on this last gathering of our six-day shamanic training, I am dressed in my best clothes: a long blue cotton dress with a white butterfly pattern. Surrounded by Nature and her pristine elements of earth, air, water, and the fiery heat of summer, I feel in harmony and at peace.

We gather around the altar circle, where Hank lights the candle placed in his carved wooden bowl, a sacred bowl of light given to him by his Hawaiian *Kahuna* mentor, Hale Makua. This is to remind him and us that in releasing all the stones that accumulate in our bowls, our hearts, we allow the light of the universe to shine brightly once again—including from our *aumakua*, our oversoul.

Part Two

Hank places the bowl of light on his prayer cloth encircled by his sacred necklace of seedpods. He brings a special collection of sacred stones, small carvings, and amulets from his travels, particularly in Africa, and shares their stories and significance. We receive the fruits of his lifelong shamanic practices gathered from the Yoruba people of Nigeria, visionary experiences in Africa's Great Rift Valley, and Hawaiian mysticism.

We place our sacred stones, necklaces, ornaments, and medicine bundles in concentric circles around his pieces. Next to these we carefully lay our drums and rattles, while we form an outer circle around the walls of the yurt.

Hank shares the healing ceremony process and our roles. He notes that all present who suffer from illnesses will be honored and receive the group's healing energies. Turning to me, he chooses me as the main recipient of healing. I feel incredibly honored and rather nervous as the "newbie" of the 22 many long-term, experienced shamanic and healing practitioners present.

Hank briefly shares my story: critical hypertension and thirteen years of complex illnesses, the initial seven spent mostly in a bedroom, being declared Totally and Permanently Disabled with chronic fatigue and common variable immune deficiency. This means my body cannot make protective proteins called antibodies to prevent many diseases, and I require monthly infusions of these immunoglobulins. I have a one percent chance of remission or recovery.

Despite changing psychosocial and spiritual aspects of my life, training as a counselor, and working as a wounded healer, I was far from healed. My ceremonial intention is to reduce my hypertension and become completely free of hospital visits for immunoglobulin treatments.

"Let's beat this thing for good!" says one circle member bluntly, and I agree.

Lying down on my back on the floor, my feet almost touch the inner altar, with my head facing outward. Hank stands close by, armed with his drum and rattle. Lady River, his trusted shamanic assistant, is on my right side near my head and heart. Kris, my partner all week, is on my left to assist River. Hank instructs me on what I will do. Although my heart quickens, I feel awe about what's ahead, and total trust in Hank and the shamanic journeying skills we all have built together this week.

Hank opens our circle with rattling, welcoming and thanking the guardian spirits of Breitenbush for their healing powers. He invokes the River Goddess and Pele, the Goddess of Fire—originally present in Hawaii, but also nearby in Mount Jefferson. Welcome and thanks also go out to all the spirits that have lived here for thousands of years, the American Indian tribes, the spirits of air, fire, water, and earth, the Nature Spirits, and the Stone Clan. After invoking the added sacred directions of Above, Below, and Within, Hank walks around the circle, rattling over each person and their hearts, to open us fully to form bridges to the Spirit Worlds.

Addressing Hale Makua, now in Spirit, Hank repeats the invocation "to lift all restrictions" while the sacred circle is open. He intones as a prayer the three *kapu*, or golden rules that Hale Makua insisted we honor; Love all that you see with humility, live all that you feel with reverence, and know all that you do with self-discipline. He also invokes Hale Makua to lead and direct the healing.

Hank begins drumming, and circle members follow suit, drumming and rattling slowly. The sounds build into a louder, powerful rhythmic beat whose vibrations enter my body and magnify. Joining our aligned hearts and spirits is the sound of ancient American Indians singing and playing drums and flutes, as if in the distance. Their spirits have often joined our ceremonies in their own individual timbres, dynamics, and flourishes, like a symphonic stereo from other worlds.

Listening to the drumming, I drift into a deeply relaxed state and visualize my familiar sacred garden, my place for pursuing visionary shamanic experiences, where I commune with my spirit guides, and my *aumakua*.

Part Two

Tonight, I invite Hale Makua and the healing spirits Hank has invoked to come forward to help me.

Surrendering to the spirits, I scan my body for all my negative thoughts, emotions, and actions needing to be released and forgiven, and my illnesses, distortions, fears, and pains—particularly emotional pain toward my ex-husband and my family of origin. The thoughts and emotions have solidified in my body and muscles as frozen fear and tight knots of fiery flames, and a hurt in my heart so that it can no longer regulate its beat. My body aches and has become immobilized with these pains, unable to fight or protect itself. I visualize my spirit helpers melting my fear, calming my heart, and "sucking up" the debris of it all. Continuing to scan my body from head to toe, I ask for cleansing and purifying.

Afterward, I call on my *aumakua* to breathe in new power, to re-empower me, to ensure all healing energies stay. Trauma, disharmony, and fear have led to losing parts of my soul and power loss. I am calling the lost soul parts back to me. The power appears as a glorious blue light descending into my body, which floods into my hair, face, teeth, bones, and down through my throat, chest, heart, lungs, stomach—and particularly my spleen, where antibodies are made. The light continues down through my spine, pelvis, and legs that support me to my feet. I see my blood that carries nutrients and antibodies turning blue from the cleansing and renewal. I feel I am soaking in a glorious blue bath of both sky and water, the Heavens and the earth at once.

Feeling stronger, I intuitively switch to a similar process of invoking the green healing light and energies of physical restoration, as well as soaking my emotional body, mental body, energetic body, and spiritual body in the light. The soaking expands outward to include all the beautiful trees and lush greenery of Breitenbush as I join with Nature and Her great healing powers, thanking Her for all that she gives to nurture and support my life.

While floating in the glorious light, Nature and Her spirit animals show themselves to me: Hummingbird, who infuses my heart with love, courage, strength, and new joy; Butterfly whose delicate wing movements of air and spirit around me help in releasing my past and give the hope and promise of transformation; Deer, who returned in an earlier soul retrieval, and now gazes lovingly with beautiful gentle eyes, her nose tenderly nuzzling my chest, reminding me that she will still protect and guide me with compassion.

Reconnecting with my *aumakua*, I relax into a deep state of peace, grateful for my oversoul's love, care, and guidance throughout my long, painful journey. I wrap myself in my *aumakua's* cocoon, filled with its unconditional love for me, and rest—until the process deepens and my body shivers and shakes uncontrollably. Surrendering to the healing energies, I lose consciousness.

When I awake, Lady River is leaning over my head and body, weaving with her hands, and blowing into my heart with cupped hands. Kris is holding my feet, pulling the energies down through my body. I slowly sense the warmth and movement of bodies surrounding me as my circle, their drums and rattles working in unison, directs the energy into me and out to the night air and beyond.

Reconnecting to my body, I send gratitude out to my spirit helpers, all the elements and guardians, Hale Makua, and those present. I dedicate my healing and send the love I have received to my three sons. The circle's drumming is attuned to me and fades with the lingering energies. A silence falls within our yurt, and I am held in a beautiful, loving embrace, as the sounds of the river and the night birds softly infuse the space.

River and Kris relax beside me, as River tells me she has blown Hummingbird medicine into my heart and woven blue butterflies into my etheric body to help with transformation, just as I had visualized. On my way to Breitenbush, I bought two paintings by an Indigenous artist in Vancouver of hummingbirds and butterflies feeding on flowers, a beautiful validation of what was to come. I share this with River as a validation of her attunement with me.

Part Two

Members of the circle and Hank validate seeing the changing-colored lights around me matching what I experienced during the healing stages. I thank everyone for their love, support, and gifts, and Hank closes the circle with prayers and thanks to all the spiritual helpers.

Saying farewell to River the next day, she hands me a raven feather as a talisman that she found outside her door. Feeling renewed, reinvigorated, and blessed, I return home.

Four months later, my immunologist reduced my monthly antibody treatments to the minimum amounts allowed, with the treatments ending within a year. Six months after my healing, I am discharged from my cardiac specialist, requiring only minimum hypertension medications. I continue to make my own antibodies, and repeated hospital tests verify a normal immune system, enabling me to be discharged permanently two-and-a-half years afterward.

My health has remained stable, and I remain forever grateful to Hank Wesselman, Ph.D., who passed into Spirit in February 2021. Aloha Hank.

Debbie Irvine, MCoun

SHE WILL DREAM THROUGH US

*A*nxiety. Helplessness. Anger. Toxic news reports about mass shootings, climate change, and other insanities of the world have me gathering a few of my sacred power objects from my altar and storming off to my sacred tree.

I have established a 22-year relationship with a special elder tree in Pittsburgh by practicing an Indigenous flowering tree ceremony, after study with Indigenous grandmothers. Only, instead of seeking the tree connection to feel more grounded and realigned with higher guidance today, I am connecting through ceremony and begin a spontaneous ceremony.

From an anguished heart, I offer myself in fierce love and service to Mother Earth, blurting out the phrase that I would be a "mouthpiece" in her service. Mid-ceremony, a peregrine falcon stuns me by landing near my sacred tree and summoning with his high-pitched call. As I approach, he continues looking directly at me and calling. After a deep nod to me, the falcon flies off toward the west, still calling.

"Ahhh, it looks like my offer to be in service has been accepted."

The very next day, I receive a phone call from a Mayan grandmother, who is of the International Council of Thirteen Indigenous Grandmothers.

Part Two

She asks whether I have followed up on her most recent instructions. I admit that I have not.

"You must go experience the great Serpent Mound. You have serpent medicine, like me, Victoria. The serpent was a great teacher to the Maya. Stay centered in your serpent medicine. Walk with it. Trust," she said.

Serpents can shed their outgrown skin and grow skin anew, their "medicine teaching" of death as being a rebirth and a transformation. This teaches old ways that no longer serve us can die and be shed so that new capacities and new life can emerge.

I arrange to visit the Serpent Mound and the synchronicities and revelations began. Though I am not musically inclined, these include song transmissions arriving in unexpected ways. All express that a New Earth consciousness of unity is being revealed.

The first song arrives and is a joyful invitation into the New Earth that has inspired me to continue my endeavors:

Come weave a web with me

A Rainbow Web of harmony

Beauty for all to see

Fulfillment, joy, and ecstasy

All life expressing unity

Weaving, weaving, weaving a New Earth dream...

The second song seems to reveal a New Earth prophecy. It describes humanity transforming after painful millennia of being stuck in a consciousness focused on separation. This potent song leads me to finding three serpent-shaped stones and guides the sacred process of their necessary reunion.

The odd thing about my three stones is that each has matching, serpent-like curves; yet they came from different locations: from the great Serpent Mound, a site close to our local Sacred White Buffalo, and from my Pittsburgh power spot with my sacred tree. Amazingly, they all fit together like puzzle pieces when stacked upon each other with their serpent faces aligned.

My three serpent stones have been revealing to me that they want a reunion in a ceremony with the spirit of the great Serpent Mound in Ohio, a massive serpent effigy mirroring the celestial serpent/dragon constellation called Draco. It has been acknowledged by the mound's current Indigenous keepers, by archaeoastronomers, and by collaborative researchers that the mound is at least 5,000 years old, based on the pole star alignment during that ancient time.

The serpent stones have been revealing that each holds frequencies of the serpentine life force known as kundalini, at three levels of creation: the earth, the human, and the heavens. This is the same life force that yoga practitioners like me strive to awaken and raise in our spines, for enlightenment. These serpent stones have revealed to me that all scales of creation—including earth, human, and the heavens—are activated by this same serpentine life force. This is sometimes called *shakti* in Hinduism, which is the primordial cosmic creation energy of the universe and is a Divine Feminine force.

These revelations and New Earth songs, I am learning to trust, have arrived from an intelligence of oneness that expresses through Mother Earth and all of creation. I trust that I am to do my part in facilitating the ceremonial reunion of these three serpent stones that found their way to me.

Calling on a ceremonially adept sacred sister, Kathy, I have her escort me to the great Serpent Mound for this process. Our ceremony at sunset at the serpent head of the mound is blessed by an exquisite, detailed cloud formation of a hummingbird, which represents the medicine of joy; her head is turned in profile, displaying a long beak, and her wings spread wide open.

Our own ecstatic joy was unleashed by the ceremony as the stones reunited the serpentine kundalini life force of the earth and heavens through the bridge of conscious humans.

Part Two

Soon after the serpent stones' reunion, Kathy and I discovered something extraordinary. The human kundalini serpent stone spontaneously shattered twice in a unique "birthing" process to release twin heart-shaped stones. Each had the shape and the actual weight of a human heart, revealing their stored knowledge. Their shattering showed us a process of humanity breaking free into our hearts: out of limiting separation consciousness into the heart of unifying love consciousness. We felt awe, witnessing their display of wisdom.

By offering myself up as a mouthpiece to serve Mother Earth I discovered a consciousness of oneness that expresses through creation. Mother Earth continues to reveal her New Earth dream to me through synchronicities and revelations, which have become our common language, our intimate communion.

Victoria Hanchin

ALASKAN BLISS

The Cessna passenger plane bringing our small group to Haines, Alaska, flies low over the pale green glacial ice. We have come to create shamanic music inspired by the energies of the fall salmon spawning season. In mid-October, Haines boasts crystalline turquoise skies, the trees offer brilliant lemon yellow and gold foliage, and snow frosts the surrounding mountain peaks. The timing of our journey as part of a two-year shamanic apprenticeship is auspicious, as previous weeks had brought heavy rain, wind, and fog that had grounded all small aircraft.

Driving through Haines to purchase food and supplies, we pull over to view hundreds of birds hovering and diving along the river. As we open the rental van doors we are hit by an overwhelming stench of dying and decaying salmon. Their incredible spawning journey over, they lay strewn along the river, among shrubs, and even hanging from tree branches. Ravens, eagles, and gulls were engaged in a feeding frenzy. Three rotund brown bears rest on the opposite riverbank, clearly satiated from a salmon feast, and eyeing us with mild curiosity.

Loading our supplies and gear into the van the next day, we drive to our launching location and meet our river guide, who will transport us by airboat

Part Two

up a frigid glacial river for our week-long wilderness retreat. Our destination is a remote stretch of sandy shore along the Chilkat River, bordered on one side by dense undergrowth and an expansive forest that merges with the surrounding mountains.

The autumn sun is setting quickly behind the surrounding peaks, so we immediately start sorting and organizing food, supplies, and camping gear for our retreat week, as well as the many musical instruments, including large frame and pow wow-sized drums, gongs, and Native American style flutes.

We pitch our tents on the sandy shore along the river and form a ceremonial circle and fire pit away from the campsite; food is hung in an oversized navy duffle bag high up in a tree to deter bears. We hustle about gathering some driftwood for our nightly ceremonial fires, and soon are swallowed by nightfall and the cold.

Kneeling in the dark on the cold river stones, I prepare our dinner, my headlamp a mere pinprick in the dark. Our makeshift kitchen is well away from the comfort and safety of our campsite and the fire, where my seated companions are barely audible as their shadows dance around the flickering flames. As I cook, I clang the pots, pans, and cooking utensils loudly to alert the bears of our presence in their territory. Still, ripples of fear crawl like centipedes up my spine as I peer into the black wall of night.

Yet when we gather later around our sacred fire and the drumming rolls out like thunder, it is a mighty spirit bear that I feel in my being. I begin to hear the words of a chant ringing in my head, and sing the words, "I'm a badass bear! I'm a badass bear! I *am* a *badass bear!*"

But we did not want to offend the resident bears, and soon we were singing an honoring song to the *medicine bears*…within and without, as we co-created the ceremonial container for our retreat.

To ease my mind as I walk back to my tent in the pitch dark, I play Tibetan bells, although I have no doubt the bears know my exact movements. Tenting so close to the water was not a good idea as the damp river night air brings below-freezing temperatures. But I am too exhausted to consider moving my campsite or leaving nearby companions. I toss and turn as the chill seeps into my bones inside my sleeping bag, a hot stone brought from the fire long grown cold.

As I lay shivering and waiting for the dawn, the wind sounds like a whining moan. But it is not the wind. It is a lone wolf with a long thin howl that repeats across the vast landscape, sending an even deeper chill through my bones; not of fear, but recognition of a connection to something primal within me. I feel the hair stiffen on the back of my neck, and I want to go out and howl rather than simply listen.

A closer visitor reveals itself in the morning, as another chill courses through my body in discovering purple bear scat and bear tracks that passed right past my tent. This bear had gorged on berries and salmon and left her calling card as a reminder that this was her domain. I am grateful we had sung our medicine bear song the night before, honoring the ancestral kinship between bears and humans as spiritual allies.

Our final night in Alaska has us drumming and singing around our fire well past midnight. Wrapped in an immense canopy of stars glimmering overhead, our drumming reverberates through the night. I transition into a deep meditative chant, singing, "Come Ancestors, come! Bring your Light, Bring your Love!" as our fire glows like a star in the wilderness.

Suddenly I feel a rush of energy and an incredible lightness as an immense energetic presence fills my being. Within moments I am in an intense state of bliss and feeling of oneness with the universe, an expansive joy I've never known before.

I realize an Indigenous grandmother ancestor has responded to our call and is now offering her blessings and speaking through me in her ancient language. Her presence fills me with such bliss that tears of joy roll down my cheeks. She brings complete, unconditional love as she addresses our ceremonial gathering, individually and collectively.

Our group leader addresses me by my spirit name and commands me repeatedly to "Come back! Come back!"

Fully present that I am temporarily housing an enlightened ancestor spirit, I let my consciousness shift with the callback; the grandmother spirit quickly departs, taking the blissful, expanded state of consciousness with her.

Though disappointed that our leader had so abruptly disrupted this sacred union with Spirit, this compassionate ancestor nevertheless blessed each of us and gifted me with a profound spiritual experience.

Stepping outside of time, I had tasted infinity and experienced the bliss of Oneness with all creation through ceremonial shamanic trance music. I know this spiritual experience will help sustain me through whatever lays before me in life. I left Haines feeling blessed by her wild places, powerful animal allies, and this ancestor's spirit—gifts that will shine in my soul forever.

Deborah Shining Star

HONORING THE ANCESTORS

Flocks of blue jays had gathered outside my kitchen window, more than could be counted and many more than had appeared in the 10 years since my grandmother transitioned. They were her way of saying hello, and with the cardinals also assembled, I knew represented a gathering of the ancestors coming to usher Mom into her return to the spirit realm.

The birds came after witnessing several conversations she had had with my grandparents on the other side. But in the days before her passing, Mom also had moments of being fully conscious, suggesting a miraculous recovery might occur, and bringing on feelings of guilt for selfishly being ready for her to leave. The eldest of three daughters, I was the only one choosing to be here in her final moments. There was karma to clear so that I did not cycle through more entangled lifetimes with this woman that I had recently grown to love.

A constant shadow had haunted Mom's spirit, which neither alcohol, drugs, nor pills had ever soothed. While tending to her affairs, it became clear that the peace she desperately hungered for related to familial choices that were so much older and larger than one lifetime. There was a story she

Part Two

took to the grave, which was only revealed by tracing a wider lens. It was after her passing that I thought to ask, and wounds were uncovered that had been passed down through a lineage of women who had never answered their true calling.

In the same way, many of her choices, as a mother and daughter, had caused a ripple of pain for each daughter that I was now discovering how to unwind from. A curious part of me awakened to uncovering the many unseen layers of mystery and deep pain, to answering those questions I had never before thought to ask. It was a quest to discover who we really were, and to find out, *What stories did I inherit in my blood, inherit from those who have gone before me?*

The answers I sought started to come in a language from the unseen that seemed very dreamlike. They began to take on a life of their own, as the more I leaned in, the more the universe responded. Reclaiming my authentic dream, my authentic self, I now know occurred in three phases, and at 10-year intervals.

The first two came after I held my Nana in 1993, and Mom in 2003, during their last breaths. I experienced a healing journey that swept me into a third cycle in 2013; freedom and empowerment came after letting go of unconscious loyalties that I had held to ancestors whose struggles were not mine to carry.

This final healing began after attending my first family constellation, a body of shamanic ancestral work a missionary developed from South African Zulu tribe traditions. The room was full of people prepared to meet the shamanic energy of their ancestors. The beyond greeted me in the form of my maternal grandfather. I had forgotten about him and never knew my father; in fact, I had been excluding the men in my lineage on both sides—a blind spot that the event revealed needed to be worked on to gain wholeness.

With the palpable intensity of woundedness in that room, though, it took three years to return to another constellation gathering. During that integration period, I often felt called to visit a graveyard discovered near my apartment, where a peace met me, as if preparing me for something.

The first sign was losing my cell phone at the graveyard. During the somewhat frantic search, I heard a loud buzzing in the distance. Looking toward the bright sun above revealed a swarm of bees in the hundreds, circling above my head before leaving as fast as they had arrived.

As a medicine woman on the shamanic path, this kind of visitation from the natural world is common; but this time, my antenna was on full alert that something big was brewing. The buzzing started again as a low humming, and they again circled above me, sharing their encoded sacred song for a few seconds before setting off. I felt the ancient future and past weaving through my core, leaving me humbled at the powerful beauty just encountered from the beyond.

Later that night, a friend invited me to join her for third row, center seats to a famous psychic's event. We were among over 800 who were desperate to meet lost loved ones. The psychic noted how some of the messages he received would blend into each other, and asked us to stand only when we recognized the details as our message.

As he explained how the session would work, my intuition said *record now* on my recorder brought to remember details with.

"Imagine what your loved one has to do to align your arrival to this moment, how many times they had to be here to interface and learn how to express through the medium of this stage; that will never happen again in this way," he said. "There was a girl who never knew the love of her father, and all her life she never really made choices to step fully into her potential, all because her father never got to tell her, 'I love you.' And love is the most important thing of all the things in life."

This message came in so strong, the moment I pressed record.

"There were three shots from behind," the psychic said. "He comes from a strong Catholic family and he said, 'I am with Mom.'"

Part Two

A girl behind me stood, hijacking the message; and so it faded out because it wasn't hers. I had been ashamed to stand up and have the history of my life—and possibly uncontrolled emotions—on full display, as the father I never knew was a heroin addict.

He had spent most of his life in and out of jail. Every time my father was released, he could not function in the real world, as prison had become his uncomfortable comfort. His last breath came while robbing a liquor store and getting shot in the back three times. His ashes went in the coffin with his mother when she passed, so she could always watch over him.

Although I did not stand in that event, the gift was received deeply. My father taught me the priceless lesson of standing up when it is my time, to speak my truth. And to know that, while he could not show up for me physically, he is a powerful ally in the spiritual realm. Most especially, he reminded me that in life, love is the most important thing.

Debra Kelly

A HEALING CALL AT A MOHAWK VILLAGE

After a playful hike in the woods, my husband and I had our curiosity piqued by a historical marker on the side of the road. No structure or grand vista was in sight. Just a sign announcing that a seventeenth-century Mohawk fortification once had been in what was a field full of metal posts.

Some posts marked where the longhouses once had stood; others traced the contours of a former stockade that had protected them. A more regular grid of stakes revealed a full archaeological excavation under way, despite no traces of the land's original human inhabitants.

What was palpable while wandering into the land was a heavy sadness, and a hush fell over us. Brian decided to leave and head toward a spring that had supplied water to the village. Scrambling to catch up with him at first, I felt something call me back up to the historical site.

Two trees growing along the fence line beckoned sweetly. One was a larger, deciduous tree—its branches entirely bare now—and the other, the sapling of an evergreen. It was just three feet tall, and I sensed that the more mature tree was mentoring the younger one. Asking if I could join them, I stood in their midst in quiet meditation.

Guided afterward to walk back into the settlement, I traced its boundaries; but I found myself heading to the village's center. Instructions soon came loud and clear about what to do there: *call out to the four directions.*

Turning to the east, I opened sacred space by invoking sunrise and springtime, the element of air, and by calling to Great Eagle and Great Condor; calling out to the spirits of the south, west, and north, I also called to the below direction, and to the above. I found myself to be at the physical center of the circle, at the very nexus between heaven, earth, and the four cardinal directions. Offering myself as a channel, I waited for whatever Spirit saw fit to bring forth.

A golden pillar of light encased me, with many distinct flows of energy moving through me from the earth into my feet, and upward through the crown of my head on into the heavens. A vibration of love and feeling of song filled my being, leaving me transfixed until the energy flow slowed to a trickle. All stilled once more, as the sensation of the light subsided. Bringing the circle to a close, I stood in silence until large flocks of geese noisily flew in steady succession overhead. With each flock that passed, the atmosphere was clearing and I was being brought back into ordinary time.

Though I had been released from the spot, I stood there with gratitude a few moments more. My heart was full for having been present to channel sacred energy at the right place and time, even while being unclear why I had served as a conduit. Having participated and experienced an utter sense of love and light was enough. The rest I was happy to leave in the realm of mystery.

My husband's bright orange jacket peeked out from behind trees on the trail as he returned from the spring. His visibly lighter mood matched my buoyed spirit, and I excitedly shared that something special but mysterious had happened. He agreed to take photos of me near my new tree friends, whom I thanked for witnessing the ceremony.

I also thanked the birds for their perfect timing and for cleansing the space with the beat of their wings and mighty honks. I thanked the spring for calling to Brian with her peaceful presence, and my husband for willingly partnering in all adventures.

Most of all, I thanked Spirit for the spontaneous opportunity to hold sacred space and experience my part in the web of life.

Ysette Roces Guevara, Ph.D.

JOURNEY TO THE SHUAR

To spend much of a week with a tribe in the Ecuadorean rainforest, our guide Mary and the rest of the group fly to Quito and travel by bus to a town now called Shell after oil companies began using it as their base. A small plane over breathtaking rainforest takes us to Miasal, whose airstrip is a cleared meadow in the rainforest. Tribal Shuar families that we will spend time with help carry our luggage on foot and by canoe to our compound.

Our home camp is nestled in the forest next to a stream displaying a beautiful array of colored rocks. Our simple rooms, built in the traditional Shuar style, have slatted walls for ventilation. The thatched, waterproof roof has a double layer of wood, with leaves in between and on top. There's also a central meeting room with hammocks, benches, and seats made from tree stumps.

In its center is a continually smoldering fire made with three logs which is the Shuar way of creating and expressing balance. Wanting us U.S. tourists to feel at home, they have installed Western style toilets, but their pipes empty directly into the rainforest.

Part Two

My senses sharpen after being here a while, and the sights, sounds, smells, and feel of the rainforest seem to permeate my whole being. Yet a sense of linear time all but vanishes. My problem-solving ability seems to go with it. I feel awkward, too, trying to communicate with the other group members, blurting out nonsensical things. Finally, I give up trying to talk, as does my roommate, who says she feels the same way.

The heightened senses are help and hindrance during a strenuous walk to thermal falls that the mother of our guide, Peem, had discovered while hunting wild boar a few years back. It is two falls side by side, one boiling hot and one icy cold.

The walk feels like a combination of mountain climbing, a high-ropes course, and a white-water rafting trip. Except instead of harnesses, life jackets, and buses at the end to drive us back, we rely solely on our Shuar guides who have their hands full as we stumble over rocks and through mud and streams in our rubber boots. We are taught to periodically empty our boots by leaning forward and bending our knees. And an extremely patient guide, when I am staggering and lurching, takes my hand, permitting me and others to smoothly go across ravines and rock ledges, up steep cliffs, and through rapids. I learn if that strong Shuar hand is holding mine, I have strength and grounding with the earth.

By the time we arrive at the twin falls, tears are flowing down my cheeks from a feeling of oneness and of being in such a flow with life. I am in love with my guide, with the Shuar, with everything and everyone, with Mother Earth. Peem and Mary say we are learning trust in others—and most of all, in ourselves. They share that our guides are mainly helping build self-confidence, a magic not only on the outside, but inside us as well. Experiencing the side-by-side falls, one of which is hot and the other cold, adds to my exhilaration.

I feel distressed that this pristine beauty and the people who live in it are threatened by the oil companies. Questioning Peem on a canoe trip, he shares that several companies plan to run an oil line through the rainforest.

Building roads and homesteading will occur, which will bring slashing and burning of the rainforest. With soils that are only 8 to 12 inches deep, this means that once an area is cleared, the rainforest won't come back.

"We must dream, a different dream for the future," he says.

The sadness returns during an ayahuasca ceremony led by a local shaman. I head into the rainforest and stand under the stars, listening to frogs and crickets. Mary joins me and I speak of my feelings.

"Let the sadness move through you. It can become creativity," she says. "See if you can stay in the present and let yourself be healed by the jungle."

Among my ceremony visions that night is seeing my six-year-old self with an open heart, pining to connect to other open hearts. I see an anaconda curled into three layers and other symbols, with which I merge and become one with. The shaman's singing all night brings comfort and continued healing. However, in the morning I suddenly hear a scream from the jungle that hits my stomach and makes the hair on my neck stand on end. The shaman later shares that what I had heard was the jaguar spirit encouraging me, and that these spirits will always be with me.

We enjoy an overnight homestay with a Shuar family. Mine is with the village herbalist, Santiago. We spend the afternoon walking in the rainforest as he tells me about the plants. We put Dragon's Blood on my insect bites, and I drink from a brew of Cat's Claw which is used for many conditions including kidney and stomach problems. There is a root that is mashed and put into the water making the fish groggy and come to the surface. There are plants to ease menstruation and labor, for stomach and intestinal pain, for parasites, and for leprosy. At night the older children do their school studies by candlelight while the younger ones play. I am given my own hut next to the family longhouse. My bed is a wooden platform made high enough to keep any snakes or lizards from climbing on my body.

When I'm returned to the Shuar the next morning, it is to prepare for the trip's main event: a chonta ceremony thanking nature for the harvest and all who are present. The chonta fruit I had picked with Santiago during our return walk is placed in front of a row of bowls, where the men present cut the skin off the fruit. The women are lined up on the other side, chewing and spitting the pulp into the bowls amidst continual joking and laughter.

After dinner, we join the ceremonial singing and dancing led by several "callers," who take turns sharing songs of celebration and gratitude. They describe the hunting and gathering of the chonta fruit, and the preparation, fermentation, and drinking of the *chicha*. To dance, we hold hands and jump sideways and back and forth. Around 2 o'clock each person takes a turn throwing a ritual spear, and the *chicha* gets passed around until dawn.

I am reminded of the gifts of these rainforest people when, on the day of our departure, it barely registers that our plane doesn't arrive until mid-afternoon. As luck has it, the spirits of the serpent and the jaguar have stayed with me. But, as in the rainforest, I have little to say when people ask about my trip.

How does one explain coming home to oneself, or the opening of your heart to a very special people? What words could express the feeling of learning trust, patience, and love through such a journey? It lasted less than a week, yet the impact will stay with me always.

Dr. Bonnie McLean

THE HOUSE OF THE DANCING SPIRITS

Carefully peeling the mosquito net back, I check the rough wooden floor before stepping down onto it because I share my dieting hut or *tambo* in the Peruvian jungle with many critters. Shoes get shaken before putting them on too, as what appeared to be a prickly, dried leaf on a previous morning was a large tarantula.

As an apprentice I must bathe in the stream at dawn. Grabbing my towel, I head to the showering platform built over the water. A million mosquitos await me there, so I vigorously fling buckets of cold water around to keep them at bay. Cleaning involves no soaps or other products—only the water flowing from the earth.

A particular rhythm Luis uses on a large, hanging wooden drum signals breakfast, which I look forward to like all meals; however meager they may be, they give me something to focus on.

Thinking that Luis will consider me a good student for the many questions I have, I wait until finishing the grilled river fish and piece of boiled yucca. Heading with my empty plate to where the maestro is sitting, I start in.

"Don Luis, I have a question about…"

Part Two

He cuts me off, exhaling in apparent exasperation, his dark eyes flash at me.

"You ask too many questions, Judita! Now go back to your hut and you ask the spirits!" he says, pointing toward my hut.

Meekly and silently, I head back across the camp and climb the crude wooden ladder into my tambo for another long day. To help be receptive to the very subtle voices of spirits, the hut lacks books or music. Endless days blend into nights, as I try to remain ever alert in case a spirit takes pity on my suffering and decides to form an alliance.

"Well, maybe I'll get back under the net for a while. That'll kill some time," I say to empty space.

Lifting the blue bed net and crawling in, I meticulously tuck its edges back underneath the mattress to keep larger insects like mosquitos out. But very tiny flies and fleas still snack on my flesh while I sleep. The torture of the resulting itching is considered part of our required suffering.

Lulled by the heat into a pleasant doze, I'm rudely awakened when something smacks me sharply on the head. Fuzzy headed, I bolt upright and look around for a rat that may have fallen on me from an overhead beam. But my pillow rests against a wall, and the bed is covered by the mosquito net. Still, it felt as if someone or something had stood behind me and slapped the top of my head.

"Hello, spirits! Is that you? I'm here! Speak to me!" I call out hopefully, only to sigh at the emptiness around me.

After lunch, I climb into my hammock whose special net keeps the bugs out, so I can dream without distraction. Something rouses me to open my eyes from the reverie; a small, transparent hand is reaching through the net toward me. Startled by this, I see it vanish.

"Wait! Come back! I saw you! Do you have a message for me?"

Again, no reply, but this time, I hadn't imagined it.

With no ayahuasca ceremony tonight as a time filler, I am keenly aware of darkness arriving around seven o'clock. I can't sleep a full 12 hours. But there's really nothing to do apart from going to bed early and stepping into a repetitive dozing and waking pattern.

Awakening at some point in the dark, it feels as if something is shaking my bed. The sensation intensifies yet is unlike earthquake vibrations. Alert now, I sense very heavy footsteps running toward my little raised hut. *Who is out there in the dark?*

The tambo's ladder shakes as if someone heavy is quickly climbing it. I'd locked the trap door entry but grab my machete, just in case.

Without the door ever opening, something enters my hut, and it's something big. The air around me changes, and I notice a sort of shimmering. My visitor starts dancing around like a crazy thing, making the entire tambo shake, but I have no fear. My concern is I'll say something and chase the spirit away. I do want it to know, though, that I'm awake and ready to chat.

"Hey, I hear you there! I'm available if you want to speak."

Again, no reply; the dancing slows, and I feel the presence leave. Stirring from slumber a bit later, there is a soft calling of my name in a sweet, high-pitched voice.

Juuudyyyyy.

"Yes! I hear you! I'm awake! Please talk to me."

After waiting through silence, I lie back down in frustration. *Why won't they answer me? Do they not like me?*

Not long afterwards, the outer edge of the bed sinks as if someone had sat down. I dare to peek out through half-closed lids, but I see nothing.

There's soon a soft sound, as if someone is lying next to me in the dark. By sharpening my focus, I hear someone breathing quietly next to me. *OK, just make sure you stay on your side of the bed.*

Morning finally arrives, and I notice at breakfast that Luis looks quite tired and ask if he's OK.

Part Two

He shares that he got no sleep. "The spirits were in my room all night, bothering me, breathing on me, and keeping me awake!"

My eyes bug out and I jump up. "Me too! They came to me too!"

Now I know what I'd experienced was real, and that the spirits are finally finding me worthy.

These night visits in the jungle decades ago were early steps into becoming a *chaka warmi*, or "bridge woman" in Quechua. My courage and growing patience with such experiences gifted me with becoming a connection between the physical and spiritual worlds. I was inducted into the Amazonian Rio Napo lineage long ago as well and continue to honor their sacred practices and traditions. The ultimate gift is that my house back in the U.S has been named *Ayarunaqwasinku*, the House of the Spirit People.

Judy Lemon

RENDEZVOUS WITH SPIRIT

The directions to the energy vortex are the least specific I've ever received.

"Go down the road from here—I can't tell you how far, since my brain doesn't do distance very well—and you'll find an old-fashioned farm gate," the woman tells me. "Open the gate and drive through. But close it behind you, because you'll be on U.S. Forest Service land, and you don't want to let the cattle out. Drive across the prairie—again, I can't tell you how far—and you'll recognize the spot. Oh, and there's a fork in the road along the way. You'll figure it out."

My traveling partner and I glance at each other as I wonder: *Can I possibly find my way with these directions? Is my sixteen-year-old Honda Accord really up for being a Land Rover? And if there are cattle there—are they friendly?*

After saying our good-byes, we head left out of the driveway, the only part of the directions we are sure about.

We've been camping in Wind Cave National Park in the southern part of the Black Hills of South Dakota. The open, rolling grasslands with a few lone buffalo; the gentle, fragrant breezes; and an occasional cluster of pine trees combine to create a sweet stirring in my heart. It is all so familiar, as if the

Part Two

falling in love with this land had happened long ago for me—maybe in my childhood visits, or in some other time all together.

Some indigenous people call the Black Hills, "The heart of everything that is." It's no surprise my heart feels so at home here.

The spirit of this land has let herself be known to me over the years through dreamy visions and coincidences, often providing guidance and support. And when needed, she has planted subtle longings in me to visit again. But this time, her call to visit had been much more concrete and emphatic.

An owl had swooped down within inches of my head before landing on the peak of a nearby rooftop. Owls are rare in my Colorado neighborhood. And this one, staring down in my direction, made certain it had my full attention before hurtling from the rooftop with singular purpose and streaking in a northeasterly direction across the darkening sky.

My ceremony the next day had revealed that the owl was summoning me to the Black Hills of South Dakota. I heard the words, *An initiation from the stars awaits you there*. It was a strikingly clear message, and intriguing enough to get me here.

I will meet you at Pe' Sla on the equinox, the message had said. Despite my habitual doubts about my ability to communicate with the worlds beyond this third-dimensional veil, I planned the trip.

Pe' Sla is a large, high-mountain prairie in the middle of the forested hills. It is sacred to the Native Americans of the area. Somehow, we have made it to South Dakota, and I feel confident I'll find the exact spot I'm supposed to be. I have found the woman reported to know the way to the sacred site, who has owned land on this prairie for many years and now acts as the land's custodian, supporting the local Native Americans as they raise money to buy back other pieces of Pe' Sla.

With her vague directions in mind, we continue our quest.

A couple of miles down the road, we spot a gate on the side of the road. It's a makeshift arrangement of random-sized pieces of wood connected loosely with barbed wire; the whole gate dances and shape-shifts when it moves, and it takes both of us to maneuver it out of the way and get our car through. I'm grateful for my companion's perseverance.

Intuition is in charge now, since we are surrounded by the emptiness of rolling prairie—no road, and no obvious destination. Luckily, the only evidence of cattle today are piles of dried dung scattered about.

The Honda doesn't seem too threatened by this landscape, so we boldly inch ahead, following the slightest of what we hope are tracks in the short, dry prairie grass. Eventually, the fork appears. *Left or right?* Deciding to steer to the left, we drive on until all semblance of tracks end at the top of a knoll. *Now what?*

Strips of colorful cloth on the ground catch my eye. Then the vague outline of a small, understated medicine wheel pops out at me. I immediately know this is it—my rendezvous spot with the spirit of the Black Hills. It's almost 2 p.m., the exact moment of the true fall equinox. I have made it to my appointment!

We slowly walk to the left around the medicine wheel three times to pay our respects before asking permission to enter the circle. It's hard to stay focused on my feet when, up above, I see a 360-degree, unobstructed panorama of the sky. Even though our star, the Sun, is dominating the sky at this time of day, the presence of all the other stars lands strongly in my awareness. I imagine this place on a clear, moonless night, and it's easy to get a deeper taste of the powerful effect of the millions of stars that are joining us here.

We enter the circle with tobacco offerings in hand and no plan beyond making an offering to each of the four directions....to the earth, air, fire, and water elements. We work quickly because the energy flowing through me at the wheel's center is so intense, my body begins hyperventilating and shaking. What a rush! It's as if the energies of the stars are being funneled right through the center of this small, unobtrusive medicine wheel and into the Earth, passing through me.

I remember the words of Oscar Miro-Quesada, spoken thirteen years earlier at a Mesa Verde kiva: *A little bit is medicine, too much is poison.* His wise words encourage me to follow my impulse and leave the circle quickly once the offerings are made.

Outside the circle, my breath and heartbeat remain rapid. I drop to my knees and press my forehead against the prickly, hard prairie. As my face touches the solid Earth, I spontaneously relax and open into reverent surrender to the Mother. Then, in one beautiful moment, my heart is filled with the love that the spirit of the Earth has for all her creatures. Rising tears attempt to release the pressure in my heart that comes from the experience of being loved so enormously.

Although I now feel complete, I am being called back into the circle again. My body is much calmer now, even while stepping into the center of the wheel. The image of the medicine circle being filled with the four colors flashes in my inner vision: white, black, yellow, and red, one color embedded in each of the four quadrants. It becomes clear that I am to speak for the Mother and bless each of the four races of humanity on Earth.

Turning to the east, I say, "May all the yellow people of the Earth be blessed with peace, abundance, and well-being."

I repeat this blessing facing the south quadrant for the red people of the Earth; facing the west for the black people of the Earth; and facing the north for the white people of the Earth, asking that all people feel this peace, abundance, and well-being.

This is Mother Earth's dream today, on the fall equinox: peace, abundance, and well-being for all her children equally. And this is my initiation from the stars. Their energy has transformed and opened me into being a willing partner with the spirit of this land, able to feel her heart and dream her dreams with her today.

I am overwhelmed with gratitude for the invitation and guidance to be here. Before leaving, I grab my medicine bundle and place it in the wheel's center for a few minutes. I intend for it to receive whatever this portal wants to place within it—maybe a dose of star medicine I can use for myself or others, or maybe the special energy I'll need to dream with the Earth again in the future.

June Konopka

LOVE CASTS OUT FEAR

I stand at the foot of the mesa, trembling like a leaf in the wind. A powerful storm batters me, whipping my compulsive thinking into a frenzy. A familiar mantra begins pounding through my skull: *You're going to die, you're going to die, you're going to die.*

My father, a gang interventionist in Chicago for more than thirty years, had prepared me for a moment like this. When I asked him how he sustained his ministry—despite the grief, pain, and fear of his profession—his answer would always be the same: "When I'm afraid, I love, and that love casts out fear."

His powerful perspective was gleaned from years of direct experience, yet I never understood it. In this moment of overwhelming terror, his words seem distant and impractical.

It's my first shamanic journey. I have driven ten hours, from Chicago to Buffalo, New York, to participate in this ceremony.

Now I am completely certain that I'm going to be torn limb from limb.

Three days before today, I'd had a vision of driving off the road. In this terrifying daydream, I never made it to Buffalo; my journey ended in a pool of blood, watching through flickering eyes as the world faded away.

Part Two

I'd been full of anxiety for weeks, but this vision kicked the intensity up a notch. Any time I was quiet enough, I'd hear the words: *You're going to die, you're going to die, you're going to die.*

Now, the moment of death has arrived. I can feel it in the air as I nervously lick my lips. Whatever happens next, I will never be the same. My body is tense, my stomach twisted into knots.

I gulp, taking a deep, rattling breath. I struggle to bring my attention to the present moment. I try feeling the sensation of my back pressed against the yoga mat and make a silent vow: *I will stay present.*

My teacher turns on a drum track and begins to guide us on the journey into the *ukhupacha*, the inner world of the subconscious, where we will meet our animal ally.

I feel my sombra, my energetic double, peeling from my physical body like a sticker, beginning at the feet. A portal begins to open between my crown and my *misarumi*, which is the ceremonial centerpiece of the Pachakuti Mesa Tradition. I travel through it.

The portal opens into a dark cave. I cannot see, but sense another's presence. My sombra is tiptoeing, walking on eggshells, doing all that it can to not make a sound. Pure terror pulses through my physical body.

Suddenly, the screaming begins.

It's a bear! Oh my God, it's a bear! It's going to eat me. I'm going to die!

The screaming I can hear in my mind is so overwhelming, I feel like I've dropped out of the journey. My mind is panicking, repeating the toxic mantra, *It's a bear! I'm going to die!* as I feel my clenched body pressing into the floor.

Minutes go by this way. A deep disappointment sets in. My teacher has stopped guiding us. The drum track throbs in the background, and still, the compulsive thinking is all I hear. It's as though my journey is suspended as fear pulses through me.

I can't believe I drove all the way here, just for this, I think. *I knew it could never work. I knew nothing could help me.*

Thirteen years of substance use had led to this moment. Less than three months into my sobriety, I began using a Reiki manifestation technique to ask for healing. Surprisingly, I'm not asking for help to stay sober. I need help staying alive.

At the age of thirteen, I started a journey with United States football and ended up with head injuries, suicidal depression, and alcohol and marijuana habits. I felt I had no one who I could talk to who understood me. I certainly didn't want to tell my parents and was determined to fix things on my own. My decision not to seek help became a pattern. Self-isolating allowed the disease of addiction to run rampant in my life.

My long walk to healing started by cutting out alcohol and leaving a deeply dysfunctional, co-dependent relationship. Yet, the energy of the disease still followed me, and I compulsively used marijuana to feel better.

At age twenty-six, the pandemic finally presented me with the opportunity to be fully sober. As I practiced sobriety, I found a deep wound: I genuinely believed I didn't belong on this planet. I didn't want to exist. Addiction had been a complex distraction to keep me from facing my suicidal thinking.

Now the universe had helped bring me here, across the country, to the foot of my mesa, journeying into the *ukhupacha*. I hope it wasn't all for nothing.

Back on the mat, the pressure continues to build. I am terrified that nothing will change, and that I will be stuck with this suicidal belief for the rest of my life.

Out of nowhere, a thought flutters into my consciousness: *This is real. Trust the journey.* I take a deep breath, and my body begins to relax.

Almost instantly I drop back into the shamanic journey. The fear, which felt like solid rock, suddenly dissipates like steam. In a split second of surprise,

I see a beautiful, white polar bear standing over me. *Is this what my mind has been afraid of?*

Before my fearful mind can react, the bear drops down onto my stomach—and the universe opens before me.

My body physically jolts on the mat as I completely let go. I can see only pure, white light. A sensation of warmth, like a blanket made of ethereal energy, seeps into the deep wounds within my chest and my abdomen. The white light becomes me, and I become it—just for a moment. It's almost like recalling a distant memory, one that is sweet, loving, and delicious. It's a moment of existing again in the womb of the cosmic mother. *Oh yeah*, my mind murmurs, *this is what love feels like.*

Sobs wrack my body. Years of this distorted thinking has genuinely convinced me that the universe would be a better place without me. The more I run from this thought, the closer I am drawn toward it. I realize that my mind has been subconsciously asking a question throughout this journey of pain and addiction: *How do I keep going when I don't believe I belong here?*

Now, with the healing medicine of love flowing into me, my question is answered: *You belong here, and I love you.*

My animal ally has given me a gift of love that I never felt worthy of receiving. I've had the experience I was seeking yet wasn't able to ask for.

Still, some part of me had known: If I answer the call to healing—if I travel across the country, if I follow my intuition—my life might really change.

Sobbing like a newborn baby, I feel physical, mental, emotional, and spiritual catharsis. The moment is an answer to a lifetime of prayers. I know that I will never be the same.

I enjoy the last few moments of familiar warmth—feeling snuggled, embraced, loved, and so deeply cared for that somehow, everything becomes right in the world. Cleansing tears continue to flow as my teacher guides us out of the journey.

I sit up and transmit the experience to my animal ally medicine piece, placing it lovingly in the south of my mesa.

I then write as quickly as I can, stopping occasionally to blow my nose and wipe tears from my eyes.

At first the writing is jumbled and emotional. Gradually, a message clarifies. Long paragraphs become a concise mantra. My experience of universal love is summarized in three succinct sentences:

"Death is love. My wounds are healed by love. Love is my gift to the world."

I remember the words of my father: "When I am afraid, I love, and love casts out fear."

I finally understand him because I have experienced Divine love. My deepest fears had surfaced, and I'd written the experience off as a failure—but with a little mindful breathing and the grace and love of the universe, that fear was lifted from my body, mind, and spirit.

I experience myself as I am destined to be. I am light. I am airy. I am free.

This is not a fairy-tale ending. I am destined to face this darkness again. But I also know that self-annihilation is no longer truly an option. Love has made it impossible to believe that the universe wants me to end my life.

I have seen the face of God, if for a few fleeting moments. That face is benevolence and freedom.

It is the face of love.

William O. Fogarty

TWO MIRACLES IN ONE MIRACULOUS DAY

I was in too much pain to walk, but the Manzanita bushes had a message for me: *Take my branches.*

During my first jazz dance class, the instructor taught me to do the "jazz walk," a movement that required me to move slowly back and forth across the dance floor on the balls of my feet with my knees deeply bent. By the end of the class, my legs were like jelly. I wanted to be a good beginner student, but I did more than I should have. I had to grasp the railing along the stairs to exit and take baby steps to get to my car.

The next morning, I knew I'd injured my left leg because my first step from bed to floor caused a sharp, stabbing pain in the soft tissue behind my knee. Diagnosis: acute tendonitis. The recovery process is slow, even with complete rest, however I was unable to take time off to let my leg heal. The pain behind my knee became chronic.

I had heard the vortexes in Sedona, Arizona helped heal you in many ways, so off I went with a friend. I have always loved nature. Its beauty makes me feel closer to God. A Sedona vortex called Boynton Canyon was known to possess both female and male energies. We decided to stop there.

Part Two

Because of my injury, I did not plan on hiking and sat on a boulder to soak in the energies and beauty right at the base of the trail instead.

"Go ahead and hike without me," I told my friend. "I'll be here."

As he slowly started up the path, I noticed the beautiful, strong manzanita bushes standing along both sides at the base of the trail. There was no way I could make the full trek further into the vortex, due to the stabbing pain that still imprisoned me. Yet how I wished I could…

Clearly, out of nowhere, I heard a voice coming from the first bush on the left, at the start of this trail. It was speaking to me! My inner ear heard it say, *Take my branches.*

I reached out and took one step while grabbing a branch for support. It felt secure and strong. Step two, on my right leg, was next, so I grabbed a branch on the right. I was still hurting, but I made a successful step. I wanted so badly to be done with this debilitating injury.

On step three, I reached for the next bush on the left … and I realized the eight-month-long injury was gone!

Stunned and confused—but so happy—I called to my friend, "I am coming, wait for me."

He was surprised, and I was still uncertain about when the pain might return. I thought I'd probably experience it somewhere on the trail, but decided, *I'll cross that bridge when I come to it. For now, I'll accept this miracle from beloved Mother Nature.*

Farther up the trail, we came upon two young adult men who said they were on their way to an Indian cave dwelling where they were going to "tone." They invited us to join them. I'd never heard of toning, but they said they would teach us.

We arrived at the dwelling that had a magnificent view of this vast, red rock canyon outstretched before us. One of the men explained and demonstrated toning. Following their lead, we joined in and formed a semicircle, overlooking the canyon. Our voices blended and soared out from under the ledge of this ancient cave dwelling.

A few moments later, I glanced over to my left. The toning made me feel relaxed, and I felt my heart opening. I looked at my friend and was startled to see a vision of a large, feathered warrior headdress that stretched from his forehead to his feet and extended a foot more behind him onto the cave dwelling's sacred ground.

I was mesmerized by this clear vision and watched until it slowly faded. Not only did my beloved Mother Nature bless me with the spontaneous healing of a long-standing injury on this day, but she also left me with a past-life remembrance of my dear friend and spiritual seed-planter. He had taught me that "thoughts are things." It didn't make sense at first, but it launched me on my spiritual journey and helped me understand we were both connected emotionally to God's creations and the beauty all around us, everywhere we went.

Many years after this experience, I learned through astrology that my friend and I had a karmic tie and had been drawn magnetically together by our higher angels to complete a past life or lives we once shared. Astrology helped me understand the vision and showed me that he was the chief of a tribe in a past life. He loved me back then, as he did in this life.

Forty years later, while still on my journey, I read online that many other people had experienced flashbacks to previous lives at Sedona's Boynton Canyon vortex. Thank you, magnificent vortex, for all you've blessed me with, providing me with two mystical encounters with the natural world on a single day.

Diane E. Broitman

SINGING WITH GAIA

I had prayed for a teacher—and one had arrived. But could we join forces to make it rain?

A week earlier, I had been at a rock bottom point in my life, struggling with hopelessness, fearing I might never find the loving relationships my heart needed. Knowing my inner sickness could not be healed by modern medicine, I had cried out in despair: *Please help me! I need a spiritual teacher.*

This prayer surprised me, as it came from a deep place within. I had an extreme distrust of spiritual leaders, but something in me knew I needed to reconnect to my spirit. The prayer reflected a depleted part of my soul that was exhausted from the life I was living. It was honest and clear. When I'd finished crying, I stood up and felt a weight had lifted from me.

Within a few days, I was introduced to a shaman who was visiting the U.S. from South America. I could sense there was something in him that I had been missing, so I signed up for his workshop the following weekend.

The strange location—on a narrow street at the edge of an unfamiliar neighborhood—made me pause. I saw no commercial buildings and no place to check in. Fear began to grow in me. *This is all wrong*, I thought. *I don't even*

Part Two

know this character. I'd been told his healing style was unpredictable—but who was he? And *where* was he?

Annoyance swept over me as I parked. *I should leave. This is all too wacky. Shamans are way outside my comfort zone, and I can't tell if I'm even at the right address!*

My contact soon came out to meet me and guided me into a humble residence where I found ten people in a small waiting room. We sat patiently, well past our stated starting time. *How arrogant this one is,* I thought, *to leave us waiting so long.* I fought the urge to walk out. Something compelled me to stay.

Finally, we were led through a small garden and into a space that was well-hidden from the street and had a separate meeting hall in the back. It was a circular room filled with an arrangement of South American altar items and shamanic tools. I was dazzled by the carefully arranged, colorful South American textiles, carved wooden walking sticks, and golden figurines of gods worshiped in ancient cultures. We settled on the floor atop small cushions.

I felt transported to a healing space, a space of mystery. The feeling shifted from anxious annoyance to wonder and anticipation. Suddenly, things seemed more expansive and elevated. I was curious. *What type of ceremony might happen here?* The place felt filled with light and mystery. The smell of sage and palo santo brought me to a more relaxed state.

We sat in a circle, surrounded by an array of instruments: drums, handmade rattles, small flutes in the shapes of animals, and drums of all sizes and shapes. The shaman entered and the group became silent, fully focused on him.

He spoke briefly and with much simplicity. "It has not rained here in some weeks, so we will participate in a rain-calling ceremony."

That was the introduction. In this simple, unexpected place, under such unusual circumstances, several strangers and I would try to make it rain.

A deep drumbeat began. I was handed a rattle, which I shook slowly. We started to synch up to a slow beat together; many of us had rattles and a few played drums or other natural-sounding instruments. We began the journey.

After some minutes, once we were beginning to settle our minds and let go of the outside concerns, the shaman began his calling on a set of various drums, including congas. Not being a musician, I can't say for sure all the types of drums he used, but soon they became a tribal symphony that one could get lost in.

When the shaman began drumming, the intensity shifted to the next level. At first, he kept an even rhythm—but the tempo was slowly escalating. The shaman played his prayer from his heart, through the drums. Soon, I was entering a trance state. I watched him as his love for nature poured through him. Also, deep within me, a palpable inner power arose. It could only come from a fusion with the powerful places in nature. This was all evident to me, despite my having no previous shamanic experience.

As the music found a dance-like pace, my heart began to open. The love and gratitude I felt for life and nature and all of Gaia's beings filled me. This was a celebration! The rattles sang, the drums sang, our hearts sang. We were in deep harmony. It was unlike anything I had ever felt: pure love, connection, and purpose.

The drumbeats transported me to a deep jungle—the home of *Pachamama*, I imagined. The jungle was dark but alive, quiet but pulsing. I could practically smell the Earth in her depths, holding life and death for so much flora and fauna.

In my vision, I began to hear the little creatures—crickets, grasshoppers, and frogs—replying with their own songs. In this moment, all was one. We were fused with the jungle and living in her realm. We sang in celebration, and the beings around us sang, too.

We were saying: *We love life, we need rain to live, it is time, we need rain, we love you.* We sang to Gaia, and as the drums began to slow, I noticed my breathing again. I was seated cross-legged and looking at the others, still in their own journeys.

I gasped when the thunder cracked. It began to rain. There had been no storm in the forecast, and its arrival was awe-inspiring, but also felt so natural. It was a miracle. I felt fully alive.

The shaman stopped drumming and left the room. We were guided to leave. As I walked into the softly pouring rains, I allowed the water to caress me as I thought about life, love, water, cycles, little beings who help call the rain, and larger beings who can enchant them with their songs. I was in rapture.

I made my way back to the room I had rented so I could attend the workshop. I saw people busy, too busy to notice the miracle of the rains. Some even might be complaining about it. The world went on as usual, but I was fully changed. I had found a new paradigm regarding our potential as humans to be in a true relationship with nature. This connection was not reserved just for shamans, although some can help us reconnect with it.

I never lost the voice of nature. I knew now that I could ask and listen, and receive healing, and create smaller miracles of my own. She is always there, our first teacher, the teacher my heart was calling for: Gaia Mother. She is conscious and aware—alive in everything. She waits for our hearts to open and discover the secrets which she has to offer. She waits for us to find the keys of gratitude, celebration, and sincerity.

Anastasia Michelle

DISCOVERING THE ROBE WASHER

I had spent the most significant and profound years of my life immersed in meditation, vision quests, and spirit journeying to the non-ordinary world. One weekend, my assignment was to go on a spirit journey—a deep meditation—and ask the spirit world, "What do I need in order to remain humble?"

At this point in my studies, I found it easy to let go of my surroundings and surrender to the non-ordinary world. As I heard the sound of the drum, my spirit animal totem—Magic the horse—met me and led me to the elders and spirit guides who always show up when I seek guidance. Immediately I saw the most beautiful robe I had ever seen. It looked like something I had seen in London at the Queen's quarters—red and gold, with gorgeous jewels.

They wrapped me in this elegant robe, and I enjoyed its warmth for a moment—until they abruptly pulled it off my body and put it away. One of the elders then led me to a river, where a woman was scrubbing white robes of all sizes and shapes.

The woman turned to me and said two words: "Robe Washer!"

Part Two

When I returned from the meditation, I wrote about this vision. *What did the message mean?* I realized her words were a lesson about abundance and humility.

I believe I am connected to the infinite resources of the Earth that birthed me—as long as I keep my ego in check. My role is Robe Washer. I need to be humble enough to allow people to be who they are while remaining open to what wants to come through me—the words and experiences yet to be spoken.

As a simple Robe Washer, I can know everything and anything. I can allow what might be rather than insisting on what must be. Just saying the name "Robe Washer" brings me from an attitude of arrogance to sacred humility. I shape-shift from self-righteousness to self-right thinking. It is such an important lesson.

I realized that humility is not a word of weakness; it indicates great strength. Humility makes the space between what was and what might be a space of gratitude, magic, and miracles. Humility reminds me that I am never separated from Mother Earth and Father Sky. We are all one, all part of the woven fabric of the Divine.

Yet this vision had shown me that I still measured my value and how deeply I was loved by external conditions. Despite all my therapy and sobriety and paths of learning, I still felt that when things were going well in my life, God loved me—and if I was not manifesting wonderful things, then God did not.

Growing up, I had been forced by my family to believe in the Southern Baptist God, who did not care for me as a gay teenager. I was told I was worthless. My grandmother said, when I was almost fourteen, that she regretted my choices and she would never see me in heaven. Although I had integrated deep truths through the years, my emotional body remembered this old space of deep pain from childhood.

I began my next spirit journey to the non-ordinary reality with this question: "What do I need to always know I am loved?"

Magic, my beloved horse, was dancing! He must have known that the moments ahead would change my life forever. The same elders led me to a large, hot fire. A couple of them held each of my open hands, almost as if they were reading my palms. Someone pulled a red-hot branding iron from the fire, and I heard the sizzle as they marked each of my palms with a heart.

"You will always be loved," they said.

The hearts were meant to remind me that I had always been loved, at all times, in all situations, through all choices and conditions. "Never forget this. Never look back and question this again."

When I returned from non-ordinary reality, I knew it had worked. The emotionally wounded piece of me was healed forever. This encounter had been just the medicine I needed.

Years later, at a shaman store in Peru, I discovered a wooden walking stick with a hand carved at the end. The palm of the hand had been branded with a heart.

With my sacred name, Robe Washer, and these hearts branded on my hands, I understood a great truth about my real value, and it brought peace to my life and heart.

Temple Hayes

WHEN STONES SPEAK

I had just wanted to sit and rest for a few minutes. But when the large boulder called my name, I couldn't help but listen.

I'd always felt most comfortable out in nature. Summer days of my childhood were lost in the mysteries of a green world. The mountains of West Virginia were my playground. Wooded slopes might disguise a cave or a moonshine still. I might hear a crow's caw or a parent calling their children to come home for dinner. The narrow valley refuge was contained by the rounded backs of the ridges, which loomed like children bent over in a game of leapfrog. Where the Tug River cut through stone, I rode my bike, hung out with cousins, and was always welcomed by grandparents who lived a few miles up the road. Brown's Creek provided hours of entertainment with its tadpoles, crawdads, and the occasional snake. Nature inspired my curiosity and delight in hidden things.

I'd traveled the world after college: Africa, Bali, Greece, Italy, and Peru. My intuition grew. I devoted hours following my breath through my body, feeling into somatic contractions caused by stress until I could track the sensation of blood pulsing and light vibrating.

Part Two

Even when I settled into a "real" job in corporate America, I focused on my sense of purpose. My perspective had become global in nature. A call to bring heaven to Earth was my muse.

I met the rock while on vacation with friends in southeastern Florida. We had arrived at West Palm Beach just as a full-spectrum rainbow became the bridge between dusk and night–a show of incandescent light from end to end. Standing there, breathing in the radiance, all the tiredness from the ten-hour drive fell away.

With the balmy April weather as backdrop, we visited the beach and shared a delicious meal at a funky outdoor café. Then we decided to pay a visit to the local botanical garden where we could talk, laugh, and catch up.

We walked the trails alongside Japanese bonsai trees, elegant footbridges, and lush vegetation. The bonsais were captivating and unique, their twisted forms expressing organized and distilled potencies. All were exquisite; some were oddly fascinating. We ranged all over the place, our spontaneous conversations in contrast to the deliberate, linear design of this pristine garden. Our relationships had been forged during a four-year apprenticeship in shamanic practices, and we shared a deep affinity for nature. Yet at first, we failed to notice the spirit of this place or its *encanto*—its charm.

As we walked through the garden's featured botanical areas, I noticed a "between" space where I felt a discreet pull to slow down and pay attention. I paused, allowing the others to move ahead. A subtle wind and the rustle of leaves alerted me to the dappled light of the tree canopy off to my right. I felt a sense of connection to an essential presence behind the tree blind. The moment that connection became real, the breeze stopped. As I stood, transfixed by stillness, an infusion of energy entered me, physically and vibrationally. The air held an otherworldly luminosity that I stretched to absorb. My being and the space around me were suspended in time.

I don't know how long I stood there. There was simply a moment when it felt complete, and the spell was broken. Inhaling deeply, I acknowledged the gift offered by the unseen realm within that chlorophyll-saturated arbor and offered tobacco and cornmeal in gratitude. *Pachamama's* generosity had given me communion.

I retained the inner bridge to this other dimension as I hurried to catch up with my friends. The fairies were afoot here. This green domain provided abundant crevices and hidey places for nature spirits, as well as habitat for the stone relatives and tree beings. Quirky little creatures, some are. Others are wise; many are shy.

The four of us soon discovered what is known as *karesansui*, a Zen composition of rock arrangements and gravel or sand. We plunked our bodies down next to this dry garden where the sand simulated water currents, islands, and waves of tranquility.

A large stone called to me.

The sensation was not unlike my earlier experience in the cloistered clearing. I listened. That big ol' rock had a lot to say. It was even more conversational than my friends sitting on the other end of the stone bench!

As I gazed at the stone, different faces shape-shifted in the reflection off its surface. It reminded me of times daydreaming with clouds in a similar dance. Perhaps the rock was curious to find a human that could speak its language, or at least one willing to make the effort to track the combination of words and images.

The rock spoke of meteor showers. It told me large stones, programmed with specific energies, had been intentionally placed in various locations across our planet. These meteorites held a spectrum of possibilities. They were generated for seeding sacred spaces, it said, to uplift planetary consciousness and imprint a foundation of supportive vibrations.

I hold the intention of peace, the substantial rock in front of me said. *Others hold diverse frequencies such as lightness of being, stability, and even laughter.*

Part Two

Years of shamanic study influence my perception of life. Every step offers initiation into the ancient intelligence of the living, breathing universe. I have come to trust the reality of imaginal realms and I bow in gratitude when given a glimpse through the portal to that reality.

Robin Blaire Harman

SNAKESKINS AND RABBIT TALES

A glint of light caught my eye as I surveyed my neglected back yard. *Is that a piece of plastic?* It lay in the flowers right next to my *apacheta*, a stone altar that's part of the Peruvian shamanic tradition I practice.

I reached down to snatch up the trash but then jumped back like I had been bitten…it was a snakeskin! A snake had nestled next to my *apacheta* and shed its skin there. The delicate husk threaded out from between two stones at the base of the structure, left behind as the snake slithered eastward into the flower bed.

I stumbled backwards, mouth agape, stunned by the significance.

I was already in the midst of a massive and multi-leveled psychic death process, the likes of which I had not encountered since my divorce, many years prior. My ego was being dismantled. Multiple physical issues had popped up, including a thyroid condition. Oddly—or maybe Divinely—one of my cats was diagnosed with a thyroid condition at the same time.

My hormonal imbalances produced terrible depression. In despair, I began to question everything about my life and business. My physical difficulties kept stripping away my favorite activities: horseback riding, bicycling, yoga, sex, cardio walking, and even standing for long periods. I had been forced to slow my pace, which is not easy for an entrepreneur.

I was facing a complete overhaul of my diet—going both gluten- and dairy-free—and was already mourning the food I could no longer eat. No more cheese, Italian food, biscuits and gravy. I desperately needed comfort, but I couldn't get it from food anymore.

The universe was asking me to turn myself inside out, to empty myself completely and undergo an intense and far-reaching transition. I had been crying and screaming, wailing and grieving. On the other side of each episode, instead of relief, I just found more grief and rage.

Just managing my own self-care and daily needs had become a monumental undertaking. I felt steeped in decay and death.

When I recognized that I was entering a major cycle of shamanic death and rebirth, I had performed a lengthy ceremony to help me acknowledge the energies present. Feeling the need to honor what was moving within and without and align with the unseen realms for support, I hoped to receive guidance and direction, and to create deliberate intentions.

My guides told me this process would take some time. I had argued with God: *Have I died enough yet? Are we good? I have a lot of work to do...* But in the end, I'd committed to surrendering to my death, however long that process would take.

I chose to consciously work with the theme of pulling up the tap root of old forms and structures. I was practically trembling as I made these proclamations. It would involve releasing long-standing vestiges of the patriarchy…unhealthy energies like forcing, taking on way too much, and having ridiculous expectations. I'd spent my life "by-Godding" as in, "By God, I'm going to make this happen," and pushing myself relentlessly with an unyielding emphasis on productivity. Now I felt like my very bones were being removed, leaving me in a listless pile of goo. *Grotesquely appropriate for a shamanic death,* I thought.

Personal Quests of Communion with Nature and Creation

My husband and I had just returned from a family vacation in Indianapolis, where we got the shocking news of another death: My godfather had died unexpectedly. We had extended our visit to attend the funeral.

The snakeskin was a much-needed sign from the Universe. The tension in my heart relaxed as I felt Creator's acknowledgement encircle me like a mother's hug. *Take heart! You are in the process of transformation. Remember that on the other side of death is always rebirth. You are healing, no matter how much it hurts or how much despair you experience. Your godfather's death, as with every death, serves a greater purpose.*

All of this seemed to be encoded in ten inches of reptilian skin. My grief was being acknowledged. I felt comforted. I felt seen.

I texted a few pictures of the snakeskin to my sister. I lingered wistfully to take in the moment, gently petting the fragile skin and giving thanks for the creature that had left it. Then I resumed my yard-tending chores.

A couple of hours later, as I weeded the flower beds, I saw a flash of white at the base of one of my plants. It was another undeniable sign: a dead rabbit. Clearly, Spirit was communicating to me in a big way, although the symbolism of the rabbit wasn't as instantly apparent to me as the snake. Again, I snapped a few photos and texted my sister.

Before I could get back in the house to look up the meaning of a dead rabbit, my sister texted me back with a link to the parable of the rabbit and the witch. I knew this story but had forgotten about it.

In the story, the rabbit, who had been a powerful warrior and friend of a witch, became afraid of the witch's powers. He wanted to never see her again. The witch, who could have killed the rabbit, chose to curse him instead, saying, "From this day forward, you will call your fears, and your fears will come to you." The rabbit became known as the fear-caller.

I was dumbfounded! Yet again, the mystical realms floored me with their accuracy. I dropped to my knees in astonishment. This folktale so perfectly described what had been happening to me during my death process. That very morning, I had been "doomsdaying," mentally running scenarios of bad outcomes and berating my perceived weakness. I had told myself, *Steph, you need to get your journal and write down all of your fears so you can get them out and start dealing with them.*

Now the little rabbit had my attention. Was I fear-calling? *Is that what this death process is about?*

I had called so many fears to me that year: physical deterioration accompanied by lack of mobility, gut-wrenching depression, and slowing my life's pace to a snail's crawl. I'd given up major categories of food and exercise. Four people had died in the space of six months. I'd been falling out of love with certain aspects of my business and living with decreased income.

Losing my energy, focus, and motivation was like dying.

I've done this kind of deep work enough to know that what you think you're working with isn't always what gets revealed when you surrender to the process. As I continually peeled back layers of the onion, trying to reach the "ground-zero lesson" of this experience, something profound struck me.

All my issues—physical, emotional, mental, and spiritual—were forcing me to leave the comfortable domain of the left brain with its masculine, action-oriented energies. I was being invited to step into the womb space of the Divine Feminine.

She wanted me to soften, surrender, and trust. It was death, but also being reborn into something new. She was inviting me to do life differently. All of my well-worn, familiar tools—hyper-productivity, by-Godding, always being in action—were being stripped from me. The Divine Feminine, in her understated way, was laying a new tool set at my feet.

And I was all thumbs.

I think she knew my hard-headedness and strong will would compel me to "take that hill," even if I was heaving myself to the top of the peak with four bloody stumps. I'm embarrassed to admit that it took this much to finally get me to sit…my…ass…down. And to listen.

As I began to allow the feminine energies to restructure me on every level, I discovered a newfound grace. My overhauled diet began to clear the fog of depression and anxiety as it rebalanced my thyroid. I finally had the hip surgery I needed. I grieved for my dead loved ones. I made peace with the aspects of my business that I needed to release.

And my ten thumbs slowly began to transform into the delicate and precise instruments of Divine Feminine love and compassion for myself. Like the rabbit, I had died, and like the snake, I had shed my old skin.

By facing my fears, I was ready—once again—to live.

Rev. Stephanie Red Feather, Ph.D.

THE SNOW BUNTING

When I heard the loud thud, I knew my worst fear had come true. A bird had crashed into my window.

The extreme frost of the Icelandic winter had begun to give way to the rising sun. The sun was up for five full hours a day now! I enjoyed every hour, even when it hung low in the sky. The sun made the icicles glisten and turned the windows into mirrors.

I had been concerned that the birds I was feeding might fly into the windows, blinded by the sun. And now it had happened. I quickly checked and saw that none of my furry friends, the cats, were around and there were no footprints in the snow from cats or dogs.

The little snow bunting lay on the ground, absolutely still, under a dripping icicle. When I scooped it up, the small head rolled onto the side as if its neck was broken. In great sorrow, I took my tiny friend into the stairwell and sat down.

As the cold was so extreme, I closed the door, but I sat near it in case of a miracle. I was hoping for one, in my heart. I reminded myself of a time when my cockatiel had banged into a window and almost died. After lying

Part Two

for a while in my hand, the cockatiel had come around. Maybe we could be this lucky again.

I studied the little bird carefully and checked for injuries to its wings or its tiny feet. Nothing was broken and I found no wounds—but it was totally lifeless. The snow bunting was still a perfect, beautiful being. Its feathers were so soft and it smelled lovely.

The tiny body fit perfectly in my left hand; I carefully covered it with my right hand as if it was inside a warming bowl. I prayed for the golden light to help me rekindle life into the little bird in my hands.

I felt a tingle in my palms. My hands got warmer. The warmth spread up my arms and throughout my whole body, as if I were sitting in a sauna. Somehow, the healing energy was healing me, as well. I had experienced a shattering loss just three months earlier, but the warmth helped me to feel whole again. Simultaneously, I saw a white ray of light flash into the stairwell, engulfing us both. With it came enormous love. I felt such gratitude for the support I got. The feeling of love and wellness brought me to tears.

There I sat in the light, cradling the lifeless body of my small friend. I prayed he would get a second chance, and that we would travel through life aware of one another.

Time passed. The streets were empty. We had the moment to ourselves. Then I felt a slight movement in its tiny feet. I carefully lifted a couple of fingers and peeked into my hands. Yes, the feet were gaining life again, but the eyes were still shut.

I felt the tickle of the wings starting to move. This time, the eyes were open. I stood up and opened the door, realizing that we had been graced by a miracle. I simply waited in awe.

Suddenly, the snow bunting struggled to its feet. I felt the enormous strength in the tiny body, and I realized that it wanted to fly. I stood up and stretched my hands through the open door. For a moment, the little creature stood on my hand—and then with a sprint, it flew out into the dusk, calling out a loud, beautiful twitter. It sounded like it was greeting its friends and also thanking me for the help.

Every autumn and winter now, when the weather is nice and there is no reason to suspect a storm coming, a lovely, small snow bunting lands on my balcony banister, to give me a heads-up that a storm is on its way. Its prediction never fails.

Fewer snow buntings show up around my house because of climate change, but I feed them every winter. Only one ever lands on my balcony. I believe that it is my friend, showing me that we are blessed by being allowed to travel side-by-side through this beautiful world.

Whenever I see it, I feel deep gratitude that I was allowed to experience the majesty and magic of the existence we call life.

Agustina Thorgilsson

THE DREAM CALLING

*H*e appeared vividly in my dream, whispering from behind me. *Sister…Sister, where are you going?*

He was polite, inquisitive …and yet insistent. He hurried to catch up to me as I pursued my journey uphill along a lush path. I turned. I knew his voice, this man. I had met don Oscar Miro-Quesada Solevo many times in the waking reality of my life. I had even prayed with him in shamanic community circles and a large shamanic intensive, where I was ceremoniously initiated into the tradition. Years later, I became a sanctioned teacher of shamanism.

As I turned to see his familiar face in my dream, my anxiety grew. In the distance behind him, I saw his wife engaging deeply with a large group around an enormous, blazing fire circle as flames leapt into the air. *Ah, shamanic community*, my thoughts reminded me, treasuring the "belonging" I was witnessing.

Sister, where are you going? he queried again.

Despite my apprehension, I responded with, "I am walking this way. I need to walk this way now," and pointed to Peru, Bolivia, and the mountains and sacred sites there.

He peered into the path that stretched out before me and without speaking, he faded back to the community and fire circle as my dream ended. When I awoke, my higher self knew I was being called by the lineages of Peruvian masters—the *altomisayoks*. My rational mind reminded me of so many doubts and feelings of unworthiness, and I let the dream calling recede from my conscious awareness.

don Oscar Miro-Quesada Solevo is an *altomisayoq*. But why was he coming directly to me in a dream? A man of great status in the shamanic world, a highly respected *maestro* and *kamaska curandero* of finely honed skills. I deeply admired his wisdom, as did a large international community of shamanic followers.

I was yet to fully understand the dream calling of the ancestral lineage and how they work through the dimensions of reality that we exist in as multidimensional beings and souls. Over the next four years, I would come to understand.

In my waking reality, I fervently continued my explorations of Peru and Bolivia, traveling two to five times a year from Florida to the magical mystery of the lands I loved. They pulled me like a magnet. I walked the land, I communed and prayed with the *apus*, the mountain spirits, and I set my intentions with my *ofrendas*, my ritual offerings. I explored the *plantas maestras*—sacred plant medicines—as I paid reverence to all. I embraced every moment, feeling enormously blessed with *Pachamama* under my feet and in my heart.

I was doing exactly what I had promised don Oscar I would do. Yet within a year's time, don Oscar appeared in another dream. *Sister, where are you walking? Sister, we are over here!* And he flung his arm out and waved his entire body in the direction of the blazing fire, showing me the vast community circle again, this time with an insistence in his voice, much louder and much closer.

"Yes, don Oscar, I see you. I am walking this way."

Sister, can I walk with you? he persisted, as he simultaneously appeared on the path by my side. I was shocked and abruptly turned to face him.

"Me? don Oscar, you want to walk with me?" I was feeling imperfect, not worthy.

Yes! Please Sister, I want to see where you are walking!

Oh my gosh, I thought in dismay. *Me?*

I was so honored that he would be interested in my journey.

I acquiesced. "Yes, I will show you."

Astutely, his skilled shamanic sight peered between the veils of reality and into my life as we strolled together for a bit.

Ah Sister, I see now, he said softly, slightly bowing and honoring my soul's journey. *And when you are ready … we are waiting for you over here.* Again, he pointed to the community, fire, and his wife.

I was whisked to the blazing fire. I felt the intensity of it on my skin! My face was still burning from the heat when I awoke.

That dream visitation, that "shamanic calling," left me transfixed. I now understood the ancestors of Peru were speaking to me about much more of my soul's work.

Sister, when you are ready, we are over here. Those were don Oscar's words in my dream. The "calling" foretold my destiny within the Pachakuti Mesa Tradition, the shamanic community my soul longed for, the place of my service for the next seven generations upon *Pachamama*.

Mona Rain

THE CALL TO HEAL

The *maestro's* assistant pointed to her heart space and said, "Here is where this medicine works. This is the place of understanding."

She was trying to explain why, when I drank the ayahuasca, I felt nothing.

As we sat that Friday evening in her thatched hut in the *Centro Espiritual*, a Shipibo encampment in Peru, I recalled my long journey with ayahuasca. It had begun three years earlier in the U.S. with the help of a medicine man. Now, here I was in the middle of the Amazonian jungles, taking a deeper dive into the mysteries of sacred plant medicines.

A few weeks into my apprenticeship with a Shipibo *curandero*, I was doing my best to absorb what he was teaching about ayahuasca—but something within me was blocking the experience. I'd drunk the visionary tea a dozen times without having a mystical experience. Despite the medicinal steam, flower, and smoke-bath purifications the medicine man had ordered to clear the cognitive and emotional blocks of Western acculturation—I was an anesthesiologist with a typical life, back in the States—the mystical experience never came.

Part Two

I'd spent the first four weeks at the *Centro* in a Master Plant *dieta*—a specific protocol of restricted diet and isolation meant to connect me with the Master Plant called *Noya Rao*. To the Shipibo people, *Noya Rao* is both a "flying tree" and a connection to the Divine. As part of the *dieta*, I'd been eating only rice, lentils, and boiled green plantains, with a boiled potato or banana when I was lucky. All my food was saltless, oil-less, and spice-less. I'd been in physical isolation and silence, without any distractions like reading, music, the internet, or sexual activity. My sole focus was on my connection with the spirit of the *Noya Rao*.

Monday morning began with lessons on the Shipibo language and instruction on the art of the *icaro*—sacred songs used during ayahuasca ceremonies for healing and to help connect us with the spirit realms. As evening approached, I went through the ritual as I did every evening before the ceremony, sitting with my *Pachakuti Mesa* and asking my spirit helpers to accompany me during the ceremony. As the sun went down, I sat on the front porch of my hut to watch the sunset and listen to the symphony of the nocturnal jungle coming to life.

I donned my ceremonial clothing and packed my pipe, my *mapacho*, and *agua Florida* with me. I was ready to rock. I meandered through the jungle in the dark of the night to the communal hut at the center of the camp. The door meowed and floorboards creaked as I walked in, greeted everyone, and made my way to my place in the ceremonial space. The room was busy with prayers, the cleansing and blessings of *mapacho* smoke, and the setting of intentions for the night.

Soon I made my way over to where the *maestro* sat to consume a cup of the thick, bitter tea. The *icaros* gradually filled the silence as I nervously sat on my mat, praying that this time my experience would be different.

An hour later, I still felt nothing. In a resolute and somber state of acceptance, I thought, *If this is the way that learning will come, then I am okay with that.*

What felt like defeat was, in fact, the opening of my heart to all possibilities. I had replaced my rational ideas of how things should be with the acceptance of how things are.

As I sat in the pitch-black room with only the melodies of the *icaros* and the flickering of the fireflies—in that moment after my internal utterance of acceptance and surrender—the hut lit up. It was as if the heavens had parted to welcome me home. A legion of angels and archangels encircled the space above me, flanking the larger-than-life, God-Goddess figure that dominated the space. It was abundantly clear to me that the being before me was *Noya Rao*, the spirit of the master plant *dieta* that had been my focus since my arrival.

Noya Rao reached into its chest area and removed what appeared to be an old-time oil lamp. Every aspect of this being emanated pristine, white light, yet the details of the being's face were perfectly clear and distinguishable. *Noya Rao* stepped closer and inserted the lamp within my chest, transmitting the message: *Now you are mine, and I am yours.*

And with that *Noya Rao* disappeared, along with the legions of angels.

As I sat there, astonished, I spotted a mammoth serpent making its sinuous path toward me. I watched the magnificence of *Sachamama*—the spirit mother of the jungle—and noticed a gleaming sphere within her mouth. I could see her forked tongue darting out alongside the sphere as she appeared to be savoring the aromas of the ceremonial space.

Within moments, the mystical serpent was before me. I perceived her telling me, in a whisper: *Extend your left hand.*

Part Two

When I did, the serpent opened her mouth and allowed the sphere to roll into the palm of my hand. As this gleaming pearl touched my flesh, I heard, echoing from all directions: *Everything is alive. Everything is Spirit.*

With this vision came cosmic wisdom. It was as if life began anew. I now breathed in a magical and mystical reality, and it has framed my every waking moment since.

Rodney Garcia, M.D.

TRAVELS BEHIND THE VEIL

*B*am! I am standing alone at the tram stop when I feel a powerful blow to the left side of my head and glimpse something black out of the corner of my eye. Whatever has hit me doesn't fall to the ground but moves back into the air in front of me. Despite the dull pain, I look up.

A full-grown crow is sitting on the tram's electrical line. It stares directly at me, somehow challenging. It is terrifying. I think of Alfred Hitchcock's film *The Birds*. It's almost as if some other, more aggressive creature has possessed this crow.

The green tram, crawling forward like a caterpillar, stops in front of me offering salvation. I gratefully climb aboard; the crow stays behind and within a short time, it is just a small, black dot.

The left side of my head throbs well into the evening hours. Thoughts of the creepy crow spin inexorably in my mind. The bird's attack felt like a slap in the face from the universe. Is it a bad omen? In German culture, crows aren't well-liked and often bring news that someone has died. But what could this bird's message be? A profound fear spreads through me, right down to the tip of every toe.

Part Two

I decide to approach what is happening in a thoughtful, rational way.

The book *Medicine Cards* has accompanied me for more than twenty years. I pick it up and start reading about Crow: All sacred texts are under the protection of Crow. The Creator's *Book of Laws* or *Book of Seals* is bound in crow feathers. Crow is also the protector of the *ogalala*, or ancient records.

As I read these words, everything in my body contracts. I can't stop feeling that I'm going to be dealing with something bad. This crow, which hit me out of nowhere, doesn't want to be ignored, and so I read on: Crow is an omen of change. Crow lives in the void and has no sense of time. The ancient chiefs tell us that Crow sees simultaneously the three fates—past, present, and future. Crow merges light and darkness, seeing both inner and outer reality.

As I think about this, a memory suddenly rises of that miserable summer when I did not make it from elementary school to secondary school. We lived in Germany and I struggled with the new language. My father angrily slapped my report card and shouted, "What is this about? Religion, handwork, sports, all very good! Arithmetic and German, very bad! You will study with me all summer vacation! Basta!"

While other children were playing outside and laughing, I would sit wedged between the couch and the table every morning in the darkened living room. My father dictated, and I wrote. If I made a mistake, he would shout at me. I made a lot of mistakes. Every dictation ended with his emotional outbursts and my tears. Reading was no better; arithmetic was even worse. The further that scorching summer progressed, the more I felt like a failure. He let me know that I was a stupid daughter. I was happy when my father finally had to go back to work.

I already hated him for ruining my school break. We hadn't read a single exciting story about Ali Baba and the forty thieves. I never got to paint a picture or do anything that would have brought joy. At the age of nine, I felt worn down and exhausted. I wanted to die.

My father would shout, "You will never become anything!" and my mother would repeat that sentence like a parrot when my father was at work. I fled to the Catholic Church on Sundays for refuge. I knelt on the hard wood for a long time, ignoring the pain in my knees as I prayed for salvation and new parents, or a place in heaven—preferably soon.

"You will never become anything" has clung to me in adulthood. At every job, the employees seem to think I am a problem. Wherever I go, life gets rigid. My body grows rigid, too. One day, my left knee stopped working and my leg became crooked.

"You need a prothesis," the orthopedist explains to me and shows me an artificial joint.

But his report to my family doctor says he feels my illness is psychological. That is more than I can take. I silently cry: *Help! I need someone skilled in understanding the deeper connection between our bodies and our spirits.*

Remembering an old trick I have read about from a Russian energy healer, I write these words on a piece of paper, roll it up, wrap a red thread around it, knot it three times, and then burn the little bundle. A few days later, information about a shamanic practitioner appears serendipitously in my email inbox.

His courses seem strange and, at the same time, familiar. In one module, he teaches that shamanism can influence or modify past events.

I decide the time has come and I am ready to begin the journey behind the veil as my energy double or shadow body. I follow the instructions and immerse myself in the breath work in preparation for the *viaje con sombra*—the shadow journey.

When the journey begins, I separate from my physical body and find I am able to move unhindered through the window. An eagle owl sits on my balcony railing and winks at me to follow. It turns around and I nestle against its back and hold on tight. How soft and fluffy its feathers are! The eagle owl flies between tall pine trees in a mountainous landscape, higher and higher.

Part Two

Then it descends and drops me on a forest path. I make my way through thick bushes and find a small pond. On the other side is the house of my childhood. My father is sitting on the terrace next to a little girl. The girl is me. She looks hollow and empty; the light of her soul is barely recognizable.

The energy of this place is uncomfortable and overwhelming, and it takes all my courage to walk toward the house. I stand in front of my father, who passed away twenty years ago. I look him straight in the eye and say, "I am going to take the girl with me now. You may not keep her, and you won't get her back." Then I take the girl by the hand and lead her away while my father watches with an expressionless face.

The eagle owl is already flapping its wings in anticipation of our journey home. The little girl wraps her arms around the bird's neck, and I wrap mine around the two of them. The eagle owl flies nimbly. During the long flight back home, the girl and I merge into one.

My body trembles and a deep sob erupts from the depths of my being. It's like my rigidity has been shattered and I have been released from a dungeon. A pain begins to spread in my back, near my kidneys.

A few days later, the pain has eased. I am in awe of what I have just experienced but feel uncertain about what will happen next. Then the signs appear.

Crow has not forgotten me. I see dozens of crows walking around in a field. I find three black feathers on my path. I realize it's time to perform the last part of the ritual. The transmogrification process progresses arduously, although the moment the ash and crystal are in the water, I feel a presence and a whoosh of movement in my apartment. The lock of my apartment door clicks, and the door swings open on its own.

I've chosen a Sunday, in honor of the exquisite Sunday excursions of my childhood. The sun is shining as I walk to the river that meanders along the outskirts of town. I sprinkle the transmogrified water into the river, knowing it will eventually reach the sea, evaporate, and rise up to the clouds that move across the sky. Maybe my father is sitting there in the clouds, looking down, happy and relieved that I did this ceremony for both of us.

Once my inner child has returned, people say I look years younger. My surgeons say I've healed three months ahead of schedule and my doctor is impressed at the degree of mobility in my knee.

The most important thing for me, however, is that I have been able to let go of my terrible memories of that summer with my father. I've managed to forgive him. It feels as if a boulder has been lifted from my heart.

Armine Bonn

ETERNITY

*O*h god, my chest hurts. The bones are breaking. The cartilage is tearing. The taste of seawater in my throat saturates my tongue. My eyes drown in the sinking sun.

The jaws open to display all that devours. Devours, and it is done. There is no turning back.

That *thing* rises in my throat. All that I have ever been to my younger self materializes. My future self, dwelling alongside my present self. In the past, always knowing, always loving. Kind, forgiving and … listening. Listening. Listening. No mother on this planet has the right combined magic to match your Divine self. You may forgive her. You may forgive your mother. You may forgive yourself. Eternal.

I sit like a lump with my grandmother and my grandmother's sister, asking, "Why now?"

"We have entered *all time*," is their soft answer.

I dig my last three-leaved *k'intu* out of my bag and set it down on the pale ground between us. The old women shake their heads.

"No, child," they say. "Take it with you."

Part Two

The dark, wet walk to the ocean is medicine for my tears. Drawing them out, washing them down into the ground. The wet sand sucking at my boots says "Stay."

A heron, as tall as a man, lifts off a drifting log, circles me, and calls its ancient, croaky cry as it rises behind me into hefty maples.

The stretch of midnight sand soaked in mist is vacant save for a woman, a mitten-sized white dog, and a child's yellow, plastic bucket. Everything empty, everything full. Everything in motion. Everything stationary. Everything dark, everything light. Everything ebbing, flooding, rising, and falling. Eternity.

I pull out the last of the seven, three-leaved *k'intus* I have brought with me on this journey and now stand on the ledge of eternity, between the two towers, between the two trees, between the two wolves, between the two snakes. The portal I must pass through. This is a tough one, the hardest yet.

My spine is burning. To stay is to suffer eternally.

I feel my heart pounding in my scalp. My crown feels cold—silver-white light cold, aurora borealis cold. A quality of cold that sinks through my body like a shaft, drilling down, down, down. Sinking through my eyes, ears, throat, neck, and shoulders. Chest, heart, ribs, and spine. Arms, elbows, wrists, and hands. Hovering there…

Breasts, belly, hips, and sacrum. Thighs, knees, shins, and calves. Ankles, feet, toes, and soles. The cold dribbles out and down into the ground through sand, rock, gravel, clay, and bedrock. Down into black underground rivers, seabeds, and caves. Drilling down into root spaces, taking me with it, into open spaces, caverns and shallows, minerals, and seas. Crystal gardens and ancient forests. Deepening through layers of dense and hard matter and through that…into Gaia's open, golden, rose-colored heart.

Then I am spewed into the void, pulsating wildly. Not my heart. Something else.

"Are you a light being?" I ask into the void. I hear laughter and feel a sinking dread in my gut.

Are you? the void asks.

I am so far from home.

I hear the meaning of *eternal*. Just then, a sharp wave of metallic taste sears through me. Extremely uncomfortable, I think I might vomit.

Get on with it, cleanse a little.

I vomit up toxins, things that don't belong or are no longer mine. Dark, sticky, slimy strands like the oil spill on the beach. Hard, sharp, jabby metallic bits, like mercury left behind on a cold planet. Foul-smelling chunks of solidified gas or conglomerated pathogens. Thoughts. Ideas. Beliefs. Griefs. Sadness. Pride. Regrets.

Fears. Fears. Lots of them.

Just when it feels like forever and ever…the dragon's golden eye opens, just a tiny slit. The light streams out—the most pure, the most bright, the most golden, fresh, new light. A slice of sun after a prairie storm. All the brighter against the backdrop of heavy, thick darkness receding. All the more welcoming and all the more searing.

Light eternal pours over and through and into me. Light, cleansed and pure. Delivered by "those-who-care." Light eternal. Love's message from an ancient home, answering all questions ever asked.

Clarifying intention. Choosing, making the choice, being the key, the requirement. I choose and choose again and remember to choose eternal light. I take the step between. I step through the two towers, the two wolves, the two trees, the two snakes. I step into the portal.

Eternal.

I blow my most sacred prayers into the *k'intu* and send them into the winds.

Part Two

A white dragon covered in fine, silky feathers scoops me up and lifts me high above the scene. The *ukhu pacha* world spreads out, falling below us, offering the ability to see the pure and loyal in the lowly and humble.

I collapse in exhaustion as she carries me above the drifting sands.

"Thank you," I say. "Please help me see."

I am profoundly grateful for dragons.

Somewhere the sky touches the Earth, and the name of that place is The End. — a Kamba saying.

Nancy E. Brown

SNAKE MEDICINE

Nowhere on the spiritual retreat's website did it mention that roosters would crow in the middle of the night. That's probably for the best.

An iPhone check shows three o'clock in the morning. I wonder if any other guest hates the roosters' obnoxious crowing more than I do. I tell myself whatever happens today is going to be better. It has to be.

Because if this doesn't work, suicide is next.

Aren't these feathered monsters supposed to wait for sunrise or something like that? I can't Google for an answer without wi-fi. On the verge of tears, I plead with the universe for something that will shut them up and let me sleep. Then I realize the exotic fowl here are probably under the spiritual protection of the shaman. Maybe wishing them harm is not the smartest thing to do.

A myriad of thoughts start battling for dominance, but thankfully, a very full bladder makes it difficult to focus for long. Not wanting to deal with anything that creeps or crawls in the night, I decide to wait until there is enough sunlight before tiptoeing to the communal bathrooms on the other side of the property. After what feels like an eternity, I am mildly amused that when the sunlight is finally bright enough, the crowing roosters shut up.

Part Two

I lift the painstakingly secured mosquito net from around the bed, grateful not to find any unwanted stowaways. Pulling a dark blue poncho over my pjs and stepping into jungle-proof sandals, I quietly accept that morning routines will be different for a while. Overall, for a private shelter in the middle of nowhere, my housing is refreshingly different, perfect for quiet reflection. In addition to the bed my room holds a rocking chair, electric fan, a small bookshelf, a hammock, and a writing desk with a bench. There is no way I will become accustomed to the top half of every wall being see-through netting—but otherwise, if this is "roughing it," ancestors be praised!

The communal bathrooms feel as far away as my comfort zone; but stepping out into the jungle is soothing. Alive in a very real way, the jungle reaches out to me. The spiritual center, located in Iquitos, Peru, radiates a raw, primal energy unlike anything I've experienced before. Towering trees, shrubs, and plants bloom with flowers of yellow, red, purple, and even pink. The ground is sand—so much sand.

My bladder reminds me there will be plenty of time to slow down and "smell the roses" later, so I rush along the sandy path toward the first open bathroom door.

Washing up in the sink, I stare hard in the mirror, examining my face the way I imagine people do after a birthday. Forty-one doesn't seem so bad. Time has treated my face well, even if it's rounder than I'd like. My hair finally reaches past my shoulders and there is more white in my beard, which I genuinely don't mind.

I know there's no logical reason for my endless anger. Don't I have it all? A new, satisfying career, a place to call home, reliable car, good friends, and loving parents. Of course, I want more but I am grateful my needs are met, and my budget can afford to let me do things I want. So why do I hate everything and everyone—especially myself?

Nothing makes sense anymore except being here in the jungle to take ayahuasca in the hopes that I will die. Yes. That makes perfect sense.

Showered, dressed, and as ready to face the day as anyone, I grab a journal, pen, and thermos. I take one more look at what is home for the next thirty days and then close the door behind me. Heading toward the main lodge and hopefully a delicious, hot breakfast, this time I appreciate the scenery with more thoughtful attention. As I walk between the butterflies, parrots, and chickens—not to mention dogs of all colors, shapes, and sizes—it starts to feel like I'm in the strangest movie ever.

I wait for breakfast in an open-air, common area between the dining room and recreation center. A large, hand-woven hanging on the wall depicts two snakes circling the ayahuasca flower. Well-read books about consciousness, plant medicine, and shamanism are everywhere. And of course, a dog, some chickens, and now a cat join me as we wait for the same thing: food.

Beans, cold pasta, rice, potatoes, and plantains. Not an egg in sight and no seasonings of any kind. I notice some fruit, but I know my plant diet forbids it. Clearly, the universe wants me to spend the rest of the day meditating and journaling in my room until ceremony time.

The day whittles away. In less than an hour, I'll be knee deep in a life-changing experience. Approaching the *maloka* for my first ceremony feels like walking up to the edge of a cliff. I am a desperate seeker, ready to jump.

A circular wooden structure covered by a massive, cone-shaped roof made from dried leaves, the *maloka* looks like the nose of a rocket. Leaving my shoes by the entrance, I take a deep breath and walk in. Twenty-eight mats with pillow, blanket, and vomit bucket are equally spaced along the wall opposite where the shamans will sit. A facilitator guides me to a mat in the middle labeled "Michael R." This is my spot.

Looking around, I realize everyone here is now part of all those who have come before and all those who will come after. Our stories and energy are woven into the history of this place like an invisible tapestry.

Settling in, I splash some Florida water on and around myself. A young guy with short-buzzed hair offers to blow *mapacho* smoke over me. He lights

Part Two

a pipe and smoke billows from his lips, covering my entire body. There is something genuine in his smile that says, *I don't know who you are, but everything is going to be okay.*

With everyone settled on their mats, the time comes to receive ayahuasca. When it's my turn, I walk to where it is served and kneel. Knowing it's my first time, the shaman pours a small amount into a glass cup. I close my eyes, offer a small prayer to the Great Mother, and take my medicine. The dark liquid is warm, almost like molasses in consistency; with a fast gulp, it disappears down my throat. Then someone turns the lights off. Only the occasional flare of someone lighting a pipe full of *mapacho* can be seen.

During a meeting yesterday, the shaman had suggested I choose a mantra to stay focused. Mine is: "Ayahuasca, do what you will, just help me heal." I mean every word. I repeat it in my head. *Ayahuasca, do what you will. Just help me heal.*

Soon I feel the first sign that something is happening, a strange sensation unlike any other plant medicine I've taken. I am falling. There is no turning back. *Dear God in whatever heaven, what have I done? Oh shit! This isn't normal, something is wrong. I should call for help. Now! Scream right now for help!* But I don't scream.

Ayahuasca, do whatever you want to me, just please help me heal! Over and over in my head. *Please help me heal. Please help me heal.*

And then, as clear as any hallucination I've ever seen, I hear, "Hello."

The snake has deep yellow eyes and black scales that shimmer like rainbows. It says, "You came."

Years earlier, during a mushroom ceremony at a workshop with another shamanic teacher, the same snake had appeared. It had crawled out from a mesa and asked me, *What is wrong?*

I had explained, "I don't know what's wrong, but no matter what I try, all I want to do is die."

If that's what you truly want, then follow me, the snake had said, flashing a glimpse of what looked like the Amazon before disappearing back into the mesa.

Now I tell the snake, "You said I would find what I was looking for here." I can't tell if it's my inner voice or if I have spoken out loud. When no one rushes over to stop me, I figure it must be safe to continue hallucinating. The effects of ayahuasca hit me harder now.

Like a radio tuning to another frequency, I start hearing strange sounds like tones or chimes. *Please help my body heal. Please help my body heal. Please help my body heal.* I go within, scanning my body, and I see the snake is inside my intestines.

Opening my eyes, I become aware for a moment of two bodies on either side of me. Someone is purging, but I can't tell who. I want to help, but I'm absorbed by the squirming feeling deep in the belly. *Holy fuck, there's a snake in my small intestine!* I grab my bucket, ready to purge, but nothing comes up. I surrender the part of me needing to make sense of what is happening—but there's a damned snake inside of me.

Don't you want to die? The snake squirms and pain shoots through my stomach—and then both disappear. Everything becomes an intricate pattern of rainbow light. It feels as if giant hands are reaching into my core, into my very DNA. I'm a vibration being tuned by the universe. In my body again, I feel something is shaking. It's me, shivering uncontrollably. I surrender.

From overhead, a soft voice asks, "Are you okay?"

"Yes," I say. At least, I think I do, or maybe I nod. The figure walks away.

After some time, I become aware that shamans are singing. I am no longer shaking, but my face is wet from tears.

A facilitator approaches. "Are you ready to receive your *icaros*?"

"Yes!" This time I know for sure I say it aloud.

They help me off the mat and slowly across the floor until I'm seated before a shaman. The figure is shrouded by complete darkness; I can only sense immense power and beauty. The facilitator speaks to him on my behalf and then walks away.

His voice is soft and hard to hear over all the other *icaros* being sung, but once I have his song in my heart, I start swaying and trembling. I don't understand the words, but I do. More tears stream down my face. It's as if the song is affecting me on a cellular level. I feel removed from my body, and for one moment, I am a snake.

Splashes of floral water snap me back to earth. My *icaros* is finished. "Gracias," I say and bow before signaling for help to stand up.

Before the facilitator offers me a hand, I realize something. With a look of panic on my face, I politely ask, "Will you escort me to a bathroom—as fast as possible?"

After my bowels release what felt like a horde of vile demons, I return to the *maloka* and my mat. Ceremony continues with shamans singing and people purging until, at last, there is a sweet silence. I'm almost asleep when someone lights a single candle in the middle of the room, signaling it is over. We can leave or stay.

Still feeling the lingering effects from the ayahuasca, I brave the shadowy jungle, guided by only a tiny flashlight beam, and head back to my room.

One ceremony down, fifteen to go. I did it. I check the time: ten minutes past midnight. Only five hours have passed.

Using Florida water as bug repellent, I carefully dress for bed, turn off the lights, and secure myself under the netting. Then I play the experience over in my head.

I'm certain now. *Yes. Everything is going to be okay.*

I close my eyes and fall asleep to the sound of crowing roosters.

Michael Bluemoon Riveron

CHRYSALIS

My fire's gone out, snuffed by the rain pecking at the tarp I hope will keep me dry. I'm alone, isolated by choice, taking my *paqo wachu*—a shamanic ritual journey.

I keep my movements to a minimum, trying not to spill the tarp's growing puddles. My fingers probe the outside of my sleeping bag. It's soaked. If the rain keeps up, I'll need to dig out the space blanket to stay warm enough to get through the night. The summer solstice, here in the Adirondacks, is frigid.

Nobody knows of my whereabouts but me. Within the universe of my isolation, my family and friends exist only because I believe they do—because I want them to. The dead mingle with the living in my memories, persistent as the rain.

At the moment, I've got two choices. I can alternate between staring at nothing in the fold of the tarp, my exhalations dull against it—or I can turn to my other side and breathe the fresh air as I peer into the void outside my tarp shell. I'm the imaginal being at the heart of a cocoon, nestled in the warmth of my down sleeping bag. I'm wide awake with nothing to do but "be."

Part Two

The *paqo wachu* is a ritual journey that practitioners of the Pachakuti Mesa Tradition make in shamanic communion with their *apu*—a mountain with a living spirit. A pilgrim paying homage, makes the *pago*, or offering. Every *apu* also has its connection to its star guide, its *apu guia*. Mine twinkles in the sky above the clouds that blacken this night.

The *paqo wachu* is about surrendering to uncertainty. It involves trusting and opening to guidance on a magnificent scale, making a one-sided bargain with the unknown.

When I close my eyes, I can see that I'm but a curiosity of my soul, incarnate for moments just like this. Stuck within this momentary cocoon, struggling with the discomforts of body and mind, I fear getting wet. I strive to escape the stagnation known as patience with whispered recitations of gratitude seeking grace. I anchor my *poqpo*, my energetic umbilical tether, into the ground beneath me.

Then I break free of my chrysalis, taking to wing, my vista growing ever more stunning. I witness myself rising above my wilderness camp. I spot my tarp-covered body below, beneath the forest canopy, motionless upon the ground. I soar upon the wings of my imagining, as true as a bird's. I'm led by those of the highest esteem in the Andean tradition, avatars to the Divine.

Siwar q'enti, the ruby-throated hummingbird, hovers before me and together, we sail through the treetops, rising past the mountains to beyond the clouds. Ruby-throated hummingbirds nest to hatch their young in these mountains during the summer.

My physical being, the *paqo* in the forest—coiled like a grub in a makeshift shelter—is diminished to nothing. I become as small as the finest grain of sand my body is lying upon. Guided by the hummingbird, we fly to the upper realms of being, the glorious *hanaqpacha*, the upper world of the shamanic practitioner. I soar as a lumen of my soul while the hummingbird hovers in place. I attune to the resonant dualities that govern the man bedded on the sand below.

I am god. I am goddess. I am in awe of the beauty that is my soul, tasked with its mission of bringing light into the world through creations of my disciplined imagination, made manifest through the dexterity of my hands. I imagine what's possible—grasping at what's attainable.

I'm torn from my reverie without warning, and the languid pools of the Milky Way vanish without a splash. My cosmic swim ends with the breach of my rain-soaked sleeping bag, which presses cold and wet against my back. I'm being played by time, pinned under a tarp, trusting in the promise that the sun will rise. Right now, that promise seems unreal. I drift off.

The rushing brook swallows all other sound. The night wears on. I awake and peel back the tarp to find the rain's let up. The tarp bends and crinkles as I cast it aside.

"Hallelujah!" I breathe out, softly, the only word I've spoken since nightfall.

Lo and behold, I see stars through every break in the canopy. The sky is clear! The rain is over.

I reset my bedding, lie on my back, and look to the sky. A prominent star shines brightly through the clearing overhead. I can't name its constellation, but I see Delphinus to the right, leaping the Milky Way. A satellite crosses the sky below the star, traveling east to west, looking like a sparkling dolphin. It's also bright. I tuck that observation away as I turn to my side and easily fall asleep.

First light comes early to the summer solstice, and it's a long, drawn-out affair. This morning, I welcome its arrival.

"*Tiyayaykuy, illari!*" I announce in Andean Quechua, welcoming the rays of the dawning day, both here in camp and within myself. Starlight is fading, taken over by the rising sun. I feel the *apus* beneath me, embracing me within their massive, deep resonance. Marvelous realms thrive within their interiors. I see this. I'm but a discoverer, an early explorer of these mystical,

Part Two

multidimensional realms. In the imagining capacity of a good mind, it's possible to make seemingly unimaginable discoveries.

The morning is so chilly and damp, I'm reluctant to emerge from my warm sleeping bag. Sunlight skims the leaders of the tallest trees. After a time, I unzip my bag and enter the new day, upright, on two legs of good service.

I shiver during a bracing splash in the brook, naked. Then I'm ready to receive the highest-order gift illuminating the relationship between *paqo, apu,* and *apu guia*—the *istrilla*. The *istrilla* is made of light, representing the *apu's* spirit. I reach into the stream to grasp what I see, yet question myself as I do—am I truly guided, or is this me wanting to fulfill a teaching? I make an offering and keep the stone. Time will tell when I'm home.

I break camp and bid farewell to this *waka*, this sacred hollow that I've come to love. I walk the stream bed when the going is good, when it's not a tumble of boulders; it's far easier than bushwhacking through spruce and blowdown while shouldering my soggy gear.

A stone in the stream catches my eye. It has a shimmer unlike any others nearby. I pull it from the flow and examine it. I'm reminded of *Oumuamua*, the interstellar probe dubbed "The Scout." Its discoverers believed it to have been an interstellar object transiting our solar system. Was it a probe sent by extraterrestrials, reaching out to humanity?

I leave a hair as *mikhushanku*, an offering, and pocket the stone. I whisper, "We're onto something, you and I, *hatun willka istrilla*—great, holy light—presenting yourself when I'm not expectant or hopeful."

I'm humbled at my expanded awareness, silently acknowledging the exquisite flow of *nuna kallpa*—my soul power—in this exquisite moment of connection and affirmation.

F. Pieter Lefferts

THE LIGHT STORM

I live in an old house converted into a fourplex in the heart of my city downtown. The building has a unique energetic signature, attracting addicts and transient types. A friend and I did a ritual cleansing when we moved in, and the apartment became my sanctuary, my spiritual haven.

My apartment on the second floor has a balcony that looks out above the rooftops of my neighbors. The balcony became an extension of the apartment, a place that, weirdly enough, felt private, even though my neighbors could see me, and I could see them. It is a space where I frequently meditate and do my yoga practice, as the apartment itself is a bit small.

Nighttime was when I felt the most called to be on the balcony. I would roll my yoga mat out with some hot tea and sink into my practice, no rules or agendas; my time to be. My little family inside, doing their own thing, would leave me to myself and my private time.

One night as I was deep in my meditation practice and connection to the Divine, the cosmic energy felt electric. My body's awareness and aliveness are at an all-time high that matches what's happening in the heavens. While my family is asleep, I stay in this state for what feels like hours. After finishing my practice, I head inside and cross the quiet apartment for sleep.

Part Two

Lying in bed with my heart open, in a deep connection to the energy present—I spend a few minutes praying and reflecting. I am pulled again toward the balcony. Quietly walking in that direction, I am greeted by one of my cats who is sitting by the balcony door; she meows as if to confirm that, yes, I am being called outside.

Picking her up and petting her, I see the sky lit up with silent lightning; the streaks of light illuminate the heavens as if a far-off fireworks display occurs for a celebration behind the clouds. There's no rain, no wind, no thunder. The quiet lightning flashes in a show that feels created just for me.

Is anyone else witnessing this magnificent light show? Am I dreaming?

I step outside, and the hairs on my skin rise in response to the electricity present in the air. As tears fall from my eyes, my arms rise, and prayers of gratitude flow from my lips; with my chest open, I drink in the celestial magic pouring down. Dancing, I open myself to the gift, and a cosmic activation occurs, an energetic conversation that passes between me and the Divine. It awakens a profound feeling of oneness with all things; everything seems big and so small all at once, and in a place of no time—just unity.

Minutes pass as the sky continues to light up. The feeling of gentle and quiet, yet fierce, power activates me as it flows through my being. I intuitively step into yoga practice, my feet steady and grounded as I fluidly move from one pose to another; my body becomes the strong altar, and my yoga practice, an honoring prayer. My cats, on either side of me, serve like pillars that hold space for this sacred moment in time.

Feeling complete in my experience and conversation with the Divine, I lie on my mat, embodying a deep sense of reverence and peace. Standing, I turn and bow at the sky, looking towards the heavens once more.

A small, blue light streaks across the sky. It is unlike any other light I remember seeing before. My crown chakra blows open and my heart explodes with an emotive force. I cry again, this time in awe of the profound gift I have received: witnessing and being a part of a brief opening of the heavens. Not fully able to comprehend what has taken place, I look around at the neighborhood and notice it feels different, like a movie scene; all is quiet, just houses and rooftops, with no people roaming about.

Making my way to my bedroom, I fall fast asleep wrapped in the embrace of warmth and the love of the Divine. The feeling and imagery are still fresh in my mind and heart the morning after, though it feels like a dream.

But I soon see that my life perspective has profoundly shifted. There is an ease and a new level of trust in how I stitch together the unfolding tapestry of my life. I now know that, beyond this reality, a truth exists that my soul recognized during that night's offering of light. An activated remembrance and freedom saturate my life now; fundamentally changing the way I show up in the world. My connection to the Great Mystery has deepened, amplifying my dedication and work to the continued growth of my soul.

As part of this growth, boxes are being packed as I prepare to move. I have lived in this apartment for more years than planned, yet there is a special tie here. The entire building is empty now, except for me and my daughter.

One day a friend comments during a visit, "Looks like you were called to live in the building to clear it out energetically. Now that everyone has left and renovations are being done, you've been released."

Her comment feels like truth. Following the light no longer feels like an option now, as my path has been illuminated for the unfurling of the next chapter of my life.

Amanda Montoya

HOW THE POWER CAME

"This is your fairy godmother, pick up the goddamn phone!"

I have been screening calls while finishing up a reiki self-treatment CD, but I laugh at hearing Uncle Henry's voice and scramble to answer.

"Listen," he says, "It's gonna be cold and wet."

My stress level shoots through the roof, as I'm sure he'll cancel my vision quest this upcoming weekend. It's something I have been praying about, and physically and mentally preparing for a few months.

"Do you want to go inside the pit instead of the hill?"

Pausing, I finally say, "No, I want the hill."

He tries talking me into the protective pit again due to the rain and cold. But he reluctantly agrees when I stick with my belief that I need the hill.

The first time I'd asked for that more challenging experience was two months earlier, when I had offered him my loaded pipe filled with tobacco and herbs. He'd smoked the entire bowl and asked what I wanted.

"I'd like to go on the hill if possible. You've taken us up there for your teachings on the night sky; I've cleaned the hill in preparation for other

Part Two

people's vision quests, so I already have a relationship with it. But mainly because I'm afraid of it."

The hill was about a quarter mile walk behind his farm, whereas the vision pit was much closer. Uncle Henry was put up on the hill for his own first vision quest in 1978. I had heard stories of how scary it could be there at night, with what one person saw there making them come running off it. I wanted to be on the hill to conquer my fear and follow in the tradition.

Instead of replying directly, he starts listing what to bring, and I know by that I am good to go: 405 prayer ties and four cloth offerings, or prayer flags; a dress, blanket, sage, and my pipe; and seven helpers. Though I already knew all of this from being a firekeeper and helper for other vision questors, it is comforting to hear again. Excitement and nervousness come with realizing there will be no backing out.

Even more nerve-wracking is the intuitive hunch that I have had that I would be doing a healing on Uncle Henry during my vision quest. *Will it be a hands-on energy healing like the many times before? Am I supposed to ask him to come inside the sacred space with me?* I had been driving myself nuts with all the what ifs, and just prayed that I would clearly know what to do and when.

Friday night is spent in the ceremonial log house, but I barely slept. Too much nervous anticipation and trying to remember all the words to the songs. Saturday morning turns out to be a beautiful, sunny day. As I pray with my pipe and gaze into the fire during a morning sweat lodge ceremony, my uncle slices four small pieces of flesh from each of my arms as offerings to the Great Spirit. This sacrifice I chose to seek a fruitful vision quest and use the power from my quest to help the people—mainly, him. Although spry and agile at 82, his arthritis pains him constantly. My intention was I needed to give something in return to ask for more power on his behalf.

After the morning sweat, my uncle and my helpers ceremonially parade me around the sweat lodge in a single file before we head to the top of the hill.

A Pendleton blanket is draped over my red cotton dress for the Sun Dance, and a pipe is in hand. I am beyond excited as I enter the hill from the east, a red-tailed hawk soars above. A good first sign.

A buffalo robe is placed atop a tarp inside the small pipe tipi on the top. It is where pipes are held during the summer Sun Dance, but now might shelter me in a heavy rain. Four big cherry branches that I had helped cut the day before are planted like curved fencing in the ground, forming a rectangle around the pipe tipi. The 405 prayer ties had been wrapped around the branches to fence me in. Each tie of small pieces of black, red, yellow, or white cloth has been folded and filled with a pinch of tobacco, and they all connect along one string. Within this sacred space, they form what I jokingly call a boxing ring to protect me from bad spirits and attract good ones.

The truth as I step inside is that I feel safe and secure being boxed in. We sing the four directions' song, and my helpers and Uncle Henry disappear down the hill.

After taking in the moment, I face the west, and sing the thank you song for my beloved sky of white puffy clouds, and everything about to take place. Birds chatter incessantly; chief among them is a gray catbird, whose nonstop chatter reminds me to listen and be still. It also brings a message about communication, that I need to get moving on a book that I've been talking about writing for years.

Facing each sacred direction, I cry and pray for hours about everything and everyone I can think of. Especially for the ancestors, my helpers, and having the ceremony provide me with the power to help my uncle. It is considered more attentive to stay standing, so I ignore a desire to sit down, despite my legs and back hurting pretty badly. My arm also aches from holding up my pipe.

Out loud, I note I'm willing to suffer, and the catbird immediately flies near again, offering an encouraging sign. Other signs that I'm being supported come from visits by a cardinal, a red-winged blackbird, a bumblebee, two

Part Two

geese, crows, an ant, a cricket, a rabbit, two butterflies, and a woodpecker. When I sing the healing song to each of the directions, the wind also kicks up forcefully.

Filled with gratitude, I repeat my constant prayer to the ultimate power of the Lakota Sioux, to Grandfather: "*Tunkashila*, help me, pity me, have mercy on me, teach me."

I have a slight headache from being without my glasses, but when I sing, Sun Dance, and pray, it becomes tolerable or unnoticeable.

By late afternoon, the rain starts. Dismissing thoughts about going inside the tipi is rewarded with the most stunning rainbow in the sky. Its beautiful pattern reminds me of my healing work, as it displays the colors of the chakras. Alongside this magnificent gift, a stunning golden light covers the southeast hillside. The meadow below is simply gorgeous, and treetops are the brightest, most exquisite green color ever. As if it couldn't get any better, the most beautiful sunset offers pink, yellow, and green colors.

Nighttime brings intermittent rain that makes the prayer flags on the cherry branches flap wildly in the wind; one branch bends so far over that I expect it to come out of the ground. Faces of spirits appear in the distant rocks and trees, yet I am not scared in my boxing ring. I have a lot of physical pain as I continue to stand and pray but access my black belt warrior within.

Eventually in the fifty-degree chill of evening, I succumb to lying down on the buffalo robe. Wrapping myself up in it like a burrito, I can feel the pulse of Mother Earth coming through on my left side. The deep cold makes focus and prayer difficult, and even rocking in a fetal position fails to keep shivers and groans at bay. My inner strength is tested in the longest night of my life.

Music comes to my ears before dawn when I hear birds singing. Uncle Henry and my helpers arrive a few hours later to take me off the hill. He looks glad to see me standing outside and praying, even though it has just started raining.

I am ready for more substantial clothes and warmth, and mystified that, since Friday at midnight, I had had nothing to eat or drink. Yet I don't feel hungry or thirsty now. The sun, which comes up as a ball of red fire in the sky, is the perfect gift to end my vision quest.

"Well, are you ready to get off this hill?" my uncle says.

"Absolutely!"

As soon as he cuts the ties to the sacred space, I step out of the supernatural world and back into the everyday one. What had been a slight headache now makes my head want to explode. My helpers gather up everything on the ground and start parading me down the hill. As we cover each direction in our descent, Uncle Henry stops and prays.

"Grandfather, she made a promise and she kept it, and I want you to look at her one more time."

I feel good about what I have done and conquering my fear.

Mitakuye oyasin! "All my relations, we are all connected."

I walk by the door of the sweat lodge and its fire. My uncle takes me inside, and we have a magical sweat. I am given the traditional post-vision quest foods of cherry juice, *wasna*, made of dried meat, fat, and cherries, as well as corn and water. I share what I saw and heard, smoke my pipe, and give thanks in a state of happiness and grace. The lodge fire's rocks glow red hot, forming an image of a single big antler, which is a sign of power.

After the sweat, I get dressed and take some headache medicine, while enjoying feeling warm again. I have fun with gift offerings to Uncle Henry and my helpers as gratitude for their prayers and help.

One of my helpers told me that on Saturday afternoon while I was on the hill, they did another sweat to help me withstand the cold and rain. Everyone then headed to the sacred tree inside the Sun Dance arbor to pray and saw the same rainbow from there. Aunt Paula, I learned, said in amazement, "Look! It's the golden healing light of the Sun Dance!"

Part Two

Another helper told me of treetops glistening in gold as I had seen occur on the southeast hillside. He and the other helpers turned out to have gone into a state of bliss, with some lying down on the ground to bask in the healing light. I realized that I had seen, and possibly helped bring about, a healing light.

By staying present to the pain and the mystery of each moment of my vision quest, healing power had also come in to help my Uncle Henry, though in a way I couldn't have possibly foreseen. In the end, it was about trusting my intuition and having faith that the spirits would work out the details, and I didn't need to know how or when.

Sharon M. Sirkis

BLESSED BY INVISIBILITY

Through my apprenticeship, don Celso taught me the two skill sets required for healing. First, I needed to learn how to develop and to discipline my "imagination." In the healing arts, imagination is about constructing images through the power of the mind. With loving intention, one visualizes the patient as healthy and whole.

"Our task as *maestros*," don Celso repeatedly told me, "is to help others remember their wholeness—that they are complete just as they are."

Second, I needed to learn to work in harmony with all the powers embodied on the medicine ground. This would help me to raise the vibration, so that the image I was holding could take form and manifest. This combination of loving intention and increased vibration is what allows magic to happen. It is also what allows healing transformation to occur.

This lesson became very clear to me during one particularly arduous pilgrimage with don Celso, his son, and his son-in-law. The occasion of our expedition was the impending arrival of a group from Lima for a series of healings. Our visitors would require a significant amount of the sacred, San Pedro cactus to be harvested and prepared. This sacred plant ally is sometimes grown in people's gardens, but the most powerful and alive of these plant relatives—and those which don Celso required for this specific ceremonial, altar-based, shamanic healing event called a *mesada*—could only be found in a hidden corner of the Chongoyape Valley. This sacred site was normally about a day-and-a-half walk from his home in Salas. To be most effective, the plant needed to be harvested in an honoring way, and only after its flowers had been enticed by the numinous light of a full moon.

Unfortunately for us, this hallowed ground where the San Pedro grew happened to be accessible only by crossing through a military base. In those days, Peru was being ravaged by the radical Marxist-Leninist terrorist group known as The Shining Path, who were part of the revolutionary movement. Because of this sad situation, a nationwide, draconian curfew had been instituted, to thwart the group's heinous activities. At that time, Peru was governed by a military dictator, and a curfew imposed by martial law meant that trespassers could be shot on sight. We chose to travel stealthily, under cover of night, to avoid detection. It was the darkest time of the month, with no moon in the sky at all. My teacher had chosen this time deliberately, so that the darkness would hide our movement.

Before beginning, and all through our journey, don Celso made offerings of *cañazo*—distilled sugar cane spirits, coca leaves, and *tabaco moro*, a type of wild tobacco used by the *apus* and *wamani*. These plants are the timeless mountain guardians and tutelary spirits of this region. Don Celso invoked all his plant and animal relatives and all ancestral allies of the pre-Columbian cultures who brought forth this lineage. He asked for help to complete this sacred mission so that no harm would befall us. He offered our pilgrimage in service to healing and in the name of the Great Mystery. As he did, he trusted that all would be well.

To avoid detection, we took a very roundabout way to our destination. It was an *El Niño* year when, because of the torrential rains, mudslides had fouled the streams we had expected to drink from and wiped out the edible plants that would normally have supplemented our rations. The little bit of food and water that we had packed was quickly depleted. Where carob trees and bushes with edible berries had once stood on our path, there was only mud and parched, brown earth. All the usual landmarks pointing our way were also gone. One day's journey quickly became two as we trudged on through the barren landscape. Yet don Celso remained confident that the San Pedro cacti we sought were still standing. His *vista* kept presenting him with a vision of the *sanpedritos* with their white blossoms waving at him, calling him forward.

It was the driest, most inhospitable trek you can imagine. Finally, after two full days and one freezing night, we came upon these sacred plant allies. The cacti stood alone in an eerily lit, otherworldly landscape. The beautiful, seven-ribbed San Pedro cacti with the most exquisite white blossoms were growing on a ledge with a little rock outcropping, just as don Celso had envisioned. We were exhilarated to see them, yet completely exhausted, hungry, and thirsty. As we approached these beautiful medicine plants, don Celso suddenly told us to sit.

Don Celso told us to quiet our minds, deepen our breathing, and become invisible. He had seen with his *vista* that the military police were looking for us. They were nearby. We steeled ourselves and we stilled ourselves. We took slow, deep breaths and went within, trusting in don Celso's guidance. We had no other choice if we were to survive.

At that moment, we began hearing the rumbling of jeep motors in the distance and the barking of dogs. Don Celso told us that, no matter what happened, we were not to open our eyes, for that would break the spell that we were weaving. He told us to be alive, yet not to be present. He insisted that any disturbance of our alignment, any breach of the shared purpose and the field of unified consciousness that we were creating, would reveal where we were.

The noises came closer.

Part Two

The four of us sat motionless with closed eyes. The dogs and the army officials were upon us. The floodlights that were shining on us were so bright that I could see the luminosity through my closed eyelids. I could hear the panting and feel the warm breath of one of the dogs at my left ear.

The soldiers were saying to one another, "They must be around here."

They were walking right next to us, literally gazing into the ground where we sat. After four or five minutes, they said, "There's nobody here. Let's go check somewhere else." Then they climbed into their jeeps and drove away.

We remained motionless for a long time after they left. We were stunned by what we had experienced, afraid to utter a sound until we heard our teacher speak. When he did, he said simply, "Brothers, the light is ours. Stand up now. It's time to celebrate the protection that our beloved *sanpedritos* have bestowed upon us."

At that moment, I knew the beautiful plant relatives that had withstood the mudslides had been waiting to offer their flesh in healing service to us. They were even flowering at the time of the new moon, which is unheard of. In this way, they were also indicating their readiness to be harvested.

Because we were impeccable in our values and our integrity, the sacred plant-relatives were still standing. They had protected us from harm and were offering themselves to us because don Celso was selflessly adhering to his *kamasqa* healing path in an honoring way. With offerings of gratitude and deep trust in the power of these sacred plant allies, don Celso had shown these, our San Pedro plant relatives, the respect that is owed them, a deference that has all but been forgotten. He was honoring the traditional ways.

Our plant allies had noticed our sacrifice, our conviction, our trust in their power, and our willingness to even risk our lives in healing service to others. Thus, a positive outcome was assured.

What I learned through this experience was this: Loving intention, selfless focus, and reverent alignment with the forces and powers of nature indeed molds the material world. These skills allow us to fashion a reality suffused with magic, medicine, and mysticism.

Oscar Miro-Quesada

PART THREE

Deepening Your Shamanic Connection

But yield who will to their separation,
My object in living is to unite
My avocation and my vocation
As my two eyes make one in sight.
Only where love and need are one,
And the work is play for mortal stakes,
Is the deed ever really done
For Heaven and the future's sakes.

—ROBERT FROST

THE SHAMAN'S MEDICINE WAY

I n my shamanic healing work as a *kamasqa curandero, paqokuna* ritualist, and transpersonal psychotherapist, I have witnessed what many might call miraculous healings. The efficacy of shamanic healing is due, in part, to the holistic approach of indigenous healers. Some holistic methods are rapidly gaining favor among Western physicians.

In many ways, the native shaman has more training than most Western physicians. The number of years of training easily equals that of Western physicians, and the range of subjects covered in the apprenticeship of a shaman is in many ways broader than that of a student of Western medicine. The shaman combines the knowledge of an herbalist, a spiritualist, and a medical internist. Unlike some Western approaches, the shamanic healing process stresses the ability to listen. This includes listening to messages from supernatural spirit realms, living tribal elders and, most importantly, the patients themselves. The native healer or shaman shows undivided attention to the problems of the ill.

As the development of psychic abilities is an integral part of the shamanic focus, native healers often anticipate when illness will appear. Some are remarkable clairvoyant diagnosticians. In many cases, they can foresee and prevent an illness in progress from becoming fully manifested in a patient.

In practice, the shaman's heartfelt conviction of vocational purpose and unshakable faith in being used as a hollow bone for healing service—that is, an unimpeded channel of spiritual power—often unleashes dynamic, psychokinetic energy that positively influences the recipient. When this healing consciousness is transmitted into the patient's bio-etheric template, it can bring about what seem to be miraculous healings.

I believe it was the great alchemist-physician Paracelsus who said that all medicines are poisons and that the difference between their powers to heal or destroy lies in the dosage. But what of the person who gives the medicine? What is his or her measure? I'm truly heartened to witness the exponential growth in numbers of women and men who are integrating the ancestral cosmovision and healing lineage of Universal Shamanism into their path of right livelihood as practitioners of urban or neo-shamanism, Earth-honoring advocacy, social justice activism, energy healing, shamanic counseling, and visionary arts.

Nevertheless, any shamanic apprentice with the courage to stare reality in the face must acknowledge the perils and pitfalls of ceremonially unleashing these powerful, autonomous forces and energies. The healing energies may increase beyond the control of the practitioner, like the tale of the "sorcerer's apprentice" who sets forces in motion and then can't stop them.

The ceremonial activation and healing use of *willka hampi*—medicine spirit—always seems miraculous. It makes visible the powers that otherwise remain invisible outside the critical context of illness and suffering. It is therefore imperative for all western-acculturated apprentices of shamanism, to first and foremost, engage in deep, personal healing. Healers must transform themselves from wounded healers to master *curanderos* before they can assist others on the journey toward self-actualization.

Non-traditional experimentation with Earth-honoring ceremonies, shamanic rites-of-passage, and energetic healings has the potential to do more harm than good if they are not situated within the context of a time-proven mentorship lineage. No part can flourish at the expense of its fellows without doing damage to the whole.

Therefore, even the most loving and well-intentioned shamanic practitioner must be sure that their shamanic tradition is openly recognized and honored as part of an unbroken heritage born from ancestral, indigenous wisdom and healing practices associated with our planet's original peoples. Most important, to be effective as a cross-cultural shamanic path with relevance for the post-modern world, one's practice must be intimately aligned with the co-creation of a heartfelt sacred community—a Universal Shamanism *ayllu* or extended spiritual family.

Contemporary shamans can expand the ancestral paths of psychic awareness and spiritual wisdom to the problems of our planet. They understand that *Gaia-Pachamama* is a conscious, living being, and that all of life is interconnected in delicate and dynamic balance. They know how to awaken and tap into their psychic gifts to cultivate spiritual discernment through the development of inner vision. By aligning with the forces of nature, great healing power becomes available to them as interdependent, luminous strands in loving service to the Great Web of Life. A modern shaman serves to remind others of the natural human ability to tap into innate psychic and spiritual essence so we can consciously transform our lives.

The following wisdom transmission is a synthesis of ancestral Andean mystical teachings taught to me by my beloved *Paqokuna* mentor from Wasao, Cusco, don Benito Qoriwaman Vargas. These teachings are a conceptually distilled rendering of Peru's highland Altomisayoq shaman-priesthood lineage intended to illumine the rich, soul-animated cosmology and nature-based pantheon of ancestral Inka deities, tutelary spirits, and both seen and unseen shamanic forces and powers that suffuse the sacred landscapes of Peru's Quechua-speaking peoples.

Many of these ancestral Andean nature spirits/tutelary entities, with the exact same functional and/or formative roles, are found in numerous other indigenous cosmologies worldwide. Welcome to the Earth-regenerative, shamanic cosmos of the Andean Paqowachu—adherents to a life of sacred reciprocity with All Our Relations, seen and unseen; a path of ritually feeding our living Earth with beauty, love, and reverence.

Haylli—Praises to *Pachamama*.

THE PAQOWACHU: REVERENCE IN ACTION

Paqowachu is a path of ritual payment or ceremonial service to the species-wide well-being. It is an ancestral, spirit-mediated, shamanic tradition of Earth-stewardship practiced in the Andes since pre-Inka times by adepts of the Altomisayoq mystical path.

Paqowachu is a life path of service involving ritual payments to Mother Earth's material/seen and spiritual/unseen dimensions of being. Throughout the Andes, Amazon, and coastal desert areas of Heart Island, this mystical and shamanic path is considered a supreme honoring of *Pukllay Kawsay*—the Game of Life. The *Pukllay Kawsay* is founded upon, and must adhere to, the principles of *Santu Kamachi Qellqa,* which is spiritual law, and *Ayni*, the principle of right returns and adhering to a life of sacred reciprocity with All Our Relations.

As offered by the Intiq Churinkuna or "Children of the Sun"—also known as the Inka—to the Western world, this mystical Earth-stewardship, shamanic path is about fully awakening our human potential and evolutionary higher consciousness. It is about attaining a state of balanced, reciprocal living with all beings, seen and unseen, and fully embodying the highest human expression of lived wisdom/visionary knowledge, compassionate love/empathic feeling, and right action/industrious physical mastery, which are known, respectively, as *yachay, munay,* and *llankay.*

It is also about the three worlds in which the shaman journeys: the upper world, a transcendent realm of Divine purpose; the middle world, which is still conditioned by humankind's collective hypnotic slumber; and the lower world, the realm of shadows.

The beauty of the *Paqowachu* spiritual path is its deep connection to:

A Highly Animated Cosmos
- *T'eqse Muyu*—Fertile Seed Circle of Universal Creation
- *Pachamama*—Mother Earth
- *Mama Killa*—Mother Moon
- *Wiracocha*—Supreme Creator/Creatrix – Great Originating Mystery
- *Taita Inti*—Father Sun
- *Wilka K'uychi*—Sacred Rainbow

The Natural Elements
- *Allpa*—Earth
- *Unu*—Water
- *Wayra*—Air
- *Nina*—Fire
- *T'eqse Kallpa*—Ether
- *Qhaqya*—Lightning
- *Illapa*—Thunder

The Living Spirits of Our Natural World
- *Tirakuna*—Watchers
- *Awkikuna*—Plant and Nature Spirits
- *Malkikuna*—Tree Beings

- *Machula Awlanchis*—Benevolent Old Ones
- *Apukuna*—Sacred Mountain Deities

Developing the level of physical power, spiritual knowledge, and soul wisdom to direct the elemental forces of Mamapacha—Mother Nature—requires the dedicated revitalization of one's total self, founded upon the practices of:

- *Allpa*—Earth Sitting; the art of "sensing"
- *Unu*—Water Purifying; the art of "feeling"
- *Wayra*—Wind/Air Walking; the art of "intuiting"
- *Nina*—Fire Sunning; the art of "thinking"
- *T'eqsekallpa*—Soul Communing; the art of "presencing"

This is not just higher center work where we get lost in our intellects and metaphysical realities. This is about being real and getting something done in the world through the activation, refinement, and masterful use of our luminous body, the *Runa Kurku K'anchay*, the subsequent weaving together of one's own bubble of living energy, the *Poqpo*, and the luminous filaments of others who are awakening to the collective pulsation. This heartbeat is felt when attaining evolutionary resonance with our *Hatun Sonqo*, the Great Universal Heart. In essence, it is about awakening to our soul's purpose and following our bliss!

THE LIFE OF A *HAMPIKAMAYOQ*: FROM HOLLOW BONE TO SHAMANIC POWER BROKER

The term *hampikamayoq* in Quechua literally translates to "being a container and repository of healing power bestowed by the guardian spirit of an ancestrally revered mountain diety." The term is composed of the union of three words: *hampi*—"medicine spirit;" *kamay*—"to create;" and *yoq*—"to contain and harness." This noble appellation is reserved for a person who has survived one or more lightning strikes or an equivalent type of near-death experience in their lives. *Hampikamayoq* is a walker between worlds, a doctor of both body and soul deeply versed in the mysteries of nature and forged by the fire reserved for adepts of the Great Work. There is unimaginable creative power and healing mastery bestowed upon the person initiated into this timeless spirit-directed service path.

Walking this Rainbow Pathway of selfless, Earth-honoring ritual dedication to Gaia-*Pachamama's* well-being commonly involves the following four steps in one's spiritual evolution as a carrier of strong medicine.

THE FOUR STEPS IN BECOMING A HAMPIKAMAYOQ

STEP 1: BECOMING A VISIONARY WATCHER

Build Your Energy Base: An increased energy base equals increased efficiency and wellness, harmony, and joy. A decreased energy base leads to feelings of alienation, victimization, and disease. This is the work of fortifying your energetic constitution. To build your energy base you will practice ceremony, work your shamanic altar or mesa, commune with nature, and practice breathwork and other self-renewal processes.

Refine Your Ability to See: To become a medicine carrier you must experience the world as an animated and interconnected field of infinite probabilities. This must be more than an intellectual knowing. You must have direct, visceral experience. To develop this ability to see and sense the unseen world, you will learn to "pay attention" and explore alternate modes of consciousness with the heartfelt intention to be of service.

STEP 2: BECOMING HEART-CENTERED

Open Your Heart: The *Hatun Sonqo*, or Great Universal Heart, is the vehicle by which forgiveness and release is made possible. To live with an open heart, we must practice *Ayni*—sacred reciprocity, becoming containers of compassionate love, reclaiming our lost pieces of self, facing our shadows, and undergoing conscious emotional clearing. This is best accomplished when we define our own personal codes of honor and strive to act with integrity.

Accept a Path of Healing Service: *Ayni* is the supreme Andean concept of sacred reciprocity—"today for you, tomorrow for me." Becoming a medicine carrier means that you will have increased capacity for manifesting change in the world. While no one can define what your path should be, identifying some dream or vision of how you might be in service and balanced relationship to your family, friends, community, or the planet itself, is an important element of this work.

While I don't mean to suggest that this work will be easy, these first steps are preparatory. They work to heal us—to make us whole—so that we may choose whether to continue along this path or to put what we have learned into the service of other healing paths. One way or another, it is still medicine for the world.

STEP 3: BECOMING A SHAMANIC HEALER

Practice Energetic Healing: Learn techniques for scanning, clearing, energizing, balancing, and transmuting energy. This includes the heart-centered harnessing and delivery of *Kawsay, Samisonqoy, K'anchay, Samiumay,* and *Illanunay* energies into a client's luminous template.

Develop an Open-Ended, Creative Healing Practice: Whether you choose music, dance, art, writing, or performing, the development of some form of creative expression is essential to the recovery and integration of the wounded healer archetype and your own universal shamanic healing artistry and service dream. Manifesting your self-directed shamanic dream in the waking world is what connects you to the highest creative source.

Shamanic Journey on Behalf of Others: Whether you intercede on behalf of friends, family, or your sacred community, you will need to attain mastery in the art of soul retrievals, illness extractions, and the functions of a psychopomp. You will need to know how to perform ceremonies for sacred alignment with Mother Earth and how to perform propitiatory spirit offerings to seen and unseen dimensions of life worlds.

STEP 4: BECOMING A *HAMPIKAMAYOQ*

Accept Higher Guidance: The final step in an apprenticeship in the *Paqowachu* tradition is to make a pilgrimage to a sacred mountain. The purpose of this pilgrimage is to develop a direct connection with one's own *apu-guia*—starlight aligned sacred mountain deity and spirit guide. This *apu-guia* eventually becomes embodied as your true shamanic self, gradually taking the place of your human teacher in the waking world.

While we will be making this journey together, we may also be at different points on our paths of service. Some of us will progress at different speeds as determined by our interest, dedication, and the extent to which this work calls us. By walking this path, we enter profound non-hierarchical partnership with All Our Relations through our experience of belongingness as an *ayllu*— an extended shamanic family united in spirit. We effortlessly support each other and focus our healing power as a sacred hoop on the co-creation of Earth-honoring community capable of positively impacting our entire Gaian biosphere.

Part Three

HOW UNIVERSAL SHAMANISM PRACTITIONERS EVOLVE INTO HEALERS

Any earnest aspirant of shamanic initiation who has heeded the call of a greater power has already begun evolving into a love-empowered emissary of healing light. It is like the process of soul refinement and physical resiliency associated with becoming a *Hampikamayoq*. As you read the five principal ways of expressing your gifts as a spirit-anointed catalyst of holistic health, I strongly suggest you write down those areas you feel most accomplished in and those areas still needing improvement. Silently read them before entering your dream time for seven consecutive nights. Upon awakening, read them out loud without attachment to the outcome. This is a simple practice for enhancing your visionary alignment as a universal shamanic initiate of the Great Work.

1. **By Example**
    - Living with an open heart in reverence to our beloved Mother Earth
    - Making each gesture and act a conscious gift to the universe: "Chop wood, carry water."
2. **By Physical Mastery**
    - Working on or with mind/body systems
    - Using massage, herbs, nutrition, acupuncture, bodywork, and ethnobotany
3. **By Energetic Mastery**
    - Affecting the energy body directly
    - Clearing, aligning, energizing, and stabilizing

- Using Reiki, bioenergetics, crystals, sound, pranic healing, *Hampikamayoq* Breathwork, and the *Pachamama* Renewal Process
4. **By Divination**
    - Providing meaning and context, supplying information
    - Paying attention, listening, observing
    - Using visionary trance, dreamwork, scrying
5. **By Mediation with the Spirit World—the Unseen and Energetic World**
    - Addressing the conditions affecting the subtle energy body
    - Using heartfelt prayer, ceremony, sacred art, ritual offerings, soul retrieval, shamanic psychopomp skills, and journeying

The universal shaman as ethnospiritual healer is a specialist in areas 4 and 5 while always striving for area 1. He or she is often, but not always, capable in areas 2 or 3.

Acknowledging one's placement at the center of the universe is basic to Earth-honoring shamanic ceremonies the world over. Thus, all ritual acts sourced from reverence and gratitude for the Great Originating Mystery's presence in one's life issues forth from the center of our Being. As a life-beautifying gift of *Ayni*, it is both a flourishing of sacred space and a consecration of spirit medicine on Earth.

Each time we align in visionary presence with the perennial wisdom soul of our shamanic ancestors, a transmission and internalization of sacred power of the highest order takes place, as energy from the Above serves as a celestial salve of healing light within the Below.

Part Three

FIVE BASIC DIAGNOSTIC QUESTIONS USED BY A SHAMANIC HEALER

These are five foundational intake questions to be answered by a healer. These are most effective in healthful, transformative value if the answers are handwritten by the person seeking healing.

- What condition in my life do I want to change?
- What is guiding me to change my ways at this specific time in my life?
- What is my role in creating my present condition?
- What has living with this condition prevented me from having or doing?
- What will happen in my life when I am free from this condition?

The effectiveness of any healing is increased when the subject of the healing participates in the process and the healer facilitates a shift or change. Many therapies can bring about change, but without the subject's participation, the change is rarely stabilized and integrated.

A shamanic healer works by interceding in the unseen world on behalf of a person in need. The shaman is a transmuter of energy, taking *hucha*—heavy, dense energy produced by being out of balance in the *Kaypacha*—and ritually feeding it back into the inner planes as nourishment for the Earth and our *Ukhupacha* dimensions. They do this in service of their client and the spiritual community. Furthermore, it is of vital importance that all good people yearning to embody the life of a shamanic healer understand that one's efficacy is directly proportional to one's freedom from self. In other words, don't take yourself too seriously.

ACTIVATING SHAMANIC STATES OF CONSCIOUSNESS

We have presented a critical overview of the most relevant concepts underlying what I have termed Universal Shamanism: its spiritual powers, healing energies, types of medicine, ritual artistry, cosmology, and nature-inspired service vision. Yet we must heed the words of my beloved mentor in Peruvian *kamasqa curandersimo*, don Celso Rojas Palomino: *"Haciendo se aprende, por Dios!"* which literally translates as "By doing one learns, for God's sake!"

I therefore enthusiastically offer you the following time-proven practices designed to deepen your connection with the varied sublime healing powers and the spiritual wisdom of Universal Shamanism. Approaching these shamanic, soul-empowered practices in a mercurial and flexible spirit and child-like curiosity shall allow their full medicine virtue to become part of your beauty walk as a sacred passerby upon planet Earth. Enjoy the ride, my friends.

Part Three

EMBODYING UNIVERSAL SHAMANISM CORE WISDOM TENETS

This simple *Kaypacha*—or "Middle World"—practice is an ideal means of unifying your inner cognitive and outer sensorial grasp of universal shamanic cosmology. This can lead to the energetic awakening and internalization of untapped evolutionary potential for the spiritual maturation of your soul.

Read all nine precepts to yourself silently, and then read them aloud, slowly, mindfully, and in a spirit of meditative contemplation. Fully savor their wisdom essence as a gift of evolutionary insight and soul-empowering agency for your life. Allow their essential truth into consciousness. Allow their physical manifestation through Earth-honoring right action. Allow their inherent wisdom beauty to sanctify, strengthen, and sustain your beauty walk as a shamanic passerby upon beloved *Gaia-Pachamama—Hinayá!*

- There is no absolute truth; truth is found in all things beautiful.
- Realize you are a "passerby" doing time; learn and practice nonattachment by being in the world and not of the world.
- Using compassionate dialogue, help others renounce fanaticism and narrowness; embrace diversity and exemplify tolerance.
- Learn to penetrate and transform hatred, anger, envy, and jealousy when they are still seeds in your consciousness.
- Never utter words that can create discord and cause our community to break; always think, speak, and act in a manner that is supportive of the Great Work.
- Give up buying bottled water and eating sources of animal protein.
- Tithe a fixed percentage of your income to a visionary Earth stewardship cause; make *karma yoga*, volunteerism, an integral part of your *sadhana*, spiritual practice.

- Remember with all your heart that how you live your life makes a difference to us all. You are an interdependent, luminous strand blessed with the ability to sustain wholeness and sanctity within the Great Web of Life.
- Practice mindful breathing to come back to what is happening in the present moment.

RIGHT ACTION BORNE OF COMPASSIONATE SPIRITUAL WISDOM... UNITES!

There are five primary sacred attributes associated with Universal Shamanism ceremonial practice. By chanting or intoning each of these three times, a celestially sanctified circle around a center point is effortlessly created. With consistent practice, this deeply integrative ritual awakens a soul-empowered expression of your Higher Self, through which an exquisitely balanced, energetic interface between Self, Culture, and Nature is attained.

Familiarize yourself with these five human attributes for sacred, Earth-regenerative living by mindfully reading each one, first silently, and then aloud, allowing a full savoring of their scripted wisdom. After completing the initial familiarization, tone or chant each attribute three times. Sweetly bathe in their revealed gnostic truth, allowing the archetypal, Nautilus-like golden spiral pathway imprinted upon your immortal soul to effortlessly align with your earthly journey. After this soul-harmonizing communion with Source … all else is a cakewalk!

- *Llankay*—pronounced "yan-kai"—Right Action, Selfless Service
- *Munay*—pronounced "moo-nigh"—Unlimited Love, Deeply Compassionate Feeling
- *Yuyay*—pronounced "you-yah-eye"—Spiritual Remembering, Divine Understanding

- ***Yachay***—pronounced "yah-chai"—Higher Wisdom, Sublime Intelligence
- ***Huñuy***—pronounced "who-new-ee"—To Unite, Harmoniously Bring Together

CONSCIOUS BREATHING: AN ENERGETIC BRIDGE TO YOUR SHAMANIC COSMOS

In its primal relation to life and spirit, the breath holds unique power for all practitioners of the sacred arts. It unites the physical vessel with the ineffable, the body with spirit, the within to the without. Nothing is more central to the act of life than breath. Counterpart to the inner connection with the Great Mystery, the breath relates us constantly to the unfolding of the bios by drawing upon the same pool of life-giving air that has sustained the evolving physical presence upon *Pachamama* for countless eons.

The management of this breath is a key element in the esoteric and initiation practices of many of the world's traditions as well as many indigenous ways of life. As the carrier of that which is within to the exterior realms, the breath is the medium of prayer, supplication, and decree. On its wisps are carried not only the messages of the people but the *kawsay*—vital life force, chi, prana—that nourishes life and the practitioner. The sanctity of this omnipresent power imparts great teaching and is the first method of developing spiritual awareness within our everyday, secular existence.

The cultivation of the breath is much like the cultivation of power itself: learning how to imbibe, retain, and release medicine in proper proportion. The awareness generated through the simplicity—never to be underestimated—is regenerative to consciousness, soul, and body. A master of breath is far along the path toward mastery in her life. Allow your breath to deepen your communion with the beauty and awakened medicine of our collective body; as earth stewards, beings who have awoken to life as an act of reverence, a partnership that heals and then expands what it means to be human. May you breathe deeply, dear ones.

HAMPIKAMAYOQ BREATHWORK

The combination of breath and visualization is a powerful shamanic tool for energetically merging our individual consciousness with the Ultimate Ground of Being. Moreover, breathwork draws in energy and the ability to visualize helps to direct that energy for personal healing or for healing others. You can practice *Hampikamayoq* breathwork anywhere, but as often as possible, try to practice it outdoors. If you can sit or stand in direct contact with the Earth, you will be able to draw in noticeably more energy.

The purpose of *Hampikamayoq* Breathwork is threefold:

1. To cleanse and clear dense energy or *hucha*
2. To fortify the energy system by the deliberate intake and distribution of *Kawsay* or prana/chi
3. To make the healer a better carrier of spirit medicine

The faster you breathe, the less you'll "feel." At twenty-six breaths per minute, one can transcend pain, heat the blood, shut down ego, and vanish bodily sensations. Extraordinary human capabilities arise, yet strain and fatigue appear. Rapid breath disconnects one from the physical.

The slower you breathe, the more you'll "feel" and the greater your interaction with the universe will be. Long, slow, deep breathing is essential to opening the heart and controlling energy within your own body, as well as directing it to others. Different patterns of energy, breathing, and visualization are useful for different purposes.

It is important that when you practice breathwork you are in a comfortable position with your spine erect but relaxed. You may choose to lie down or to sit forward on the edge of your chair. If you sit cross-legged on the floor, consider using a pillow to give you proper support.

THE BREATHING PROCESS

Begin by exhaling all the air from your lungs and briefly pause before slowly inhaling to a count of ten. Retain your breath for another ten count and slowly exhale to the count of ten. Pause on the exhalation and repeat the process for ten minutes. This brings energetic balance to your physical, mental, emotional, and spiritual vehicles, forming what is known as the upward triangle of cosmic equilibrium.

THE I AM HARMONIZATION RITUAL

Wise spiritual leaders in both Eastern and Western traditions knew that vibration is creation. By extension, uttering certain frequencies can restore wholeness to a fractured being, no matter the species. So often in our daily lives, we attend to the needs of the body or of the mind, but we forget that the spirit also requires nurturing to bring us into balance. Only when body, heart, mind, spirit, and soul are all in balance can we come into more intimate contact with our Universal Self, which is a process of re-membering our wholeness. The following practice is an ideal way to come into oneness with your divinity as a shamanic beauty walker in harmonious relationship with a user-friendly multiverse.

Sit in a chair that fully supports your body and allows your back to be comfortably straight. Rest your feet on the floor, slightly apart, with your heels together and put your hands in your lap with your right hand in your left palm and your thumbs gently touching. If you have ever noticed Egyptian depictions of the ancient pharaohs, you will see this same position depicted. This position, or full body mudra, helps to anchor and harmoniously circulate vital life force energies crucial to your continued evolution as a Divine being.

Always begin this *Hampikamayoq* breathwork with a deep exhalation, emptying your lungs fully. Then, with the tip of your tongue gently touching the upper palate of your mouth, jaw relaxed, begin by taking three deep breaths through the nose, inhaling for a count of ten, retaining for a count of ten, and exhaling for a count of ten. Remember, as you breathe in oxygen, you are simultaneously crystalizing vital life force within every fiber of your being. Bring your awareness to the top of your head and pineal body, imagining and feeling a shaft of pristine luminous energy descending from the celestial realms. Experience it flowing down the length of your body and out of the soles of your feet into our beloved Earth Mother's sacred body.

On your fourth inhalation, you begin toning I AM. As you do so, remember that this toning is an offering as well as an awakening, for there is sacred reciprocity in all things. Start on any note of the scale that is comfortably low by toning aaaaaahhhhhh. This is the vowel sound that creates the vibration that opens the heart center. As you continue to vocalize, slide your voice up a full octave and let the aaaaahhhh become eeeeeeeee. Thus, you have the "I" which sounds like "aaaaaahhhh-eeeeeee."

The eeeeee sound creates the vibration that is perfectly suited to aligning with the higher realms. As you tone this sound, it gives the same vibration as that of bells, chimes, and Tibetan *tingshas*. When you have offered all your breath to this two-pitched aaahh-ee, pause and breathe. Then return to the first pitch—which is a full octave lower than the "eeee" ending of the two-pitched "I" sound you have just completed. Breathe in and tone "AM," drawing out the vowel and the consonant so that it sounds like "aaaaammm." This vocalization draws spirit into the belly, crystalizing it firmly in the physical plane.

Repeat this process, toning "I-AM" as you draw out each vowel and the "m" sound seven times to complete the practice. Complete this process at least once per day for seven days and then at least once per week for seven weeks. You will begin to feel a significantly heightened level of consciousness and a deepening of your psychic faculties and overall perception. Enjoy your Divine awakening, my beloved shamanic beauty walkers!

CONSECRATING YOUR SHAMANIC CEREMONIAL SPACE

The first act in the ceremonial unfolding of creating a healing altar or shamanic mesa is the consecration of the ground upon which it is to be placed. As a way of honoring the perfection and sanctity of life as it exists within the "now," this ritual act opens us to the greater forces of the *T'eqse Muyu*, through the power of our conscious acknowledgement of the living Universe. A centering of both ritualist and space, the consecration is the first move in the dance of relationship, which is the defining characteristic of Earth-honoring practices. Witnessing the interdependence of time and space, concentrated through the active relationship of the practitioner to the cosmos allows this unified field to serve as the anchoring point and genesis of all ceremonial conduct to follow.

- **Florida Water**—*Agua Florida*—Masculine
  The Propitiation and Ritual Feeding of *Pachamama*
- **Blue Cornmeal**—*Mama Sara*—Feminine
  The Sacred Circle or Hoop; the *T'eqse Muyu* or Living Universe
- **Tobacco**—*Sayri*—Masculine

The Sacred Equidistant Cross: Drawing together synchronic vertical time and diachronic horizontal time; a ritual merging of circular spiritual temporality and linear material temporality in consciousness
- **Coca**—*Mama Kuka*—Feminine
The integration of the three foundational worlds or *pachas*—*Hanaq, Kay,* and *Ukhu*—and the sacred attributes—*Yachay, Munay,* and *Llankay*—of Andean ethos within the shamanic lineage field of the *Mesa*

In the ecological ethos of the Andes, the act of consecration brings together female and male reproductive aspects, engendering a metabolic, complementary union that is the basis of *Mesa* cosmology and is the source of great ritual power. The encircling of the Earth with cornmeal represents the womb, with the tobacco introduced as the male member. The coca stands for the ovum that is the center of this coming together, while the Florida water indicates the semen that completes the creative joining. Out of this complementary paired holism—recreating as it does the basic generative archetypes of the *T'eqse Muyu* as seen from the eyes of the *Runa*—a transcendental totality of space and time is remembered as the foundation for ceremonial endeavor.

THE CONSECRATION PROCESS

1. *Pachamama's* thirst is satiated, and her sacred body fed by offering a few drops of **Florida water**—or any other aromatic water or clear spirits—into the center of the area where the shamanic altar is to be assembled.
2. Beginning in the South, a clockwise circle is drawn with **blue, white, or yellow cornmeal**.

3. With **tobacco**, a cross is drawn from North to South and from East to West.
4. A three-leaf **coca** or *k'intu*, prayed over, anchors all intention, and is placed in the center of the cross. Bay leaves are a good alternative to coca leaves.
5. Snapping the fingers over the *k'intu* is a gesture of "sealing the medicine" and a symbolic decree of the unified power of our consecrated intention. By placing it into the center of the ground upon which the manta is then placed, we accomplish a "squaring of the circle."

Thus, our ceremonial patterning of sacred space involves an initial offering of aromatic libation, the clockwise circle of blue cornmeal, the equidistant cross of tobacco, and the prayerful placement of a three-leaf coca k'intu upon that sacred center. This is then customarily covered by an exquisitely woven square-shaped ground cloth—a *manta* or *unkuña*.

This is an elevated use of imitative magic with dramatic impact upon the soul maturation of all parties present. Accomplishing this unmistakably esoteric Squaring of the Circle will serve as your primary universal shamanism lineage ceremonial space. Over time with discernment, you can embellish your space by adding other shamanic artifacts, power objects, and ceremonial items. The progressive addition of these medicine pieces also amplifies the experience of unitive consciousness in the life of the ritualist. This ceremonial patterning consistently replicated in ritual performance by initiates of the Great Work, shall organically begin to manifest a collective morphogenetic field of enormous bio-etheric influence ultimately becoming an unstoppable evolutionary catalyst for global human spiritualization.

Note: Before that loving nourishment is offered as a ritual feeding into *Pachamama's* Great Sacred Web of Life, each ingredient must be reverently prayed over. It is important to realize that all ritual acts borne from such a heightened state of shamanic consciousness extend far beyond the physical locality of one's service work. This level of soul-awakened service is considered a most noble blessing, a highly beneficent offering of Divine nourishment for both our universal shamanic lineage and Gaia's entire biosphere.

SHAMANIC EARTH WALK RITUAL: LIGHT — LOVE — EARTH — UNITED — I AM

This universal shamanic practice is an exquisite method for balancing spiritual and material dimensions of our human experience. When practiced regularly, it dramatically enlarges one's consciousness of being a luminous strand within Great Spirit's numinous web of sacred relationships, all of which sustain our Cosmic Mother's dreaming ways.

This is preferably done outdoors. Begin by standing with heels together and feet slightly apart, forming a V-shape. Your arms should hang at your sides, palms facing forward. Close your eyes and take three deep, centering breaths through your nose.

1. Feeling the Earth beneath your feet, take a step forward with your right foot and mentally repeat or visualize *K'anchay*, which means "light."
2. Then take a step with your left foot and mentally say or visualize *Munay*, which means "love."
3. Next, take a step with your right foot again and say or visualize *Pachamama*, the "Earth."

4. Then, bringing your left foot next to your right, with heels together and feet slightly apart forming a V-shape, mentally repeat or visualize *Huñuy*, meaning "united."
5. Finally, mentally repeat or visualize the word *Ñoqani* for "I AM."

Once this first cycle is complete, you may repeat the same five-step Shamanic Mindfulness Earth Walk cycle as many times as your heart desires.

THE *PACHAMAMA* RENEWAL PROCESS (PRP)

You can tap the soul-nurturing beauty of Mother Earth with the *Pachamama Renewal Process*. Within the rich corpus of Universal Shamanism ritual arts, this is the practice most often used as a vehicle for the invoking, evoking, and decreeing the healing power of the Earth in service to the Great Work. Performed both individually and as a group ritual, it is a supreme way of engaging the sacred reciprocity of the universe for personal and planetary benefit.

When approached with an easy state of reverence, the *Pachamama Renewal Process* swiftly attracts the benevolent attention of countless spirit-helpers from the natural world. It creates a sustained field of resonant interaction between the elemental forces of Earth, Water, Air, Fire, and Aether. This sphere of beneficent, transformational intention and evolutionary grace harnesses and uses a variety of available seen and unseen shamanic powers and natural forces in the integrative healing service of self, others, and humankind as an organismic system.

PRP RITUAL ENACTMENT

The practitioner brings hands together, thumbs and forefingers touching, to form a diamond pattern that is held over the *qosqo*—the navel area of your body. Knees are best slightly bent, with back straight but relaxed. The feet should be comfortably placed at shoulder width. An energetic filament is extended from one's *qosqo* or umbilicus into the Earth. Through deep breath and focus, resonance is established. Then the following intonations are made to draw the appropriate energies.

> **QOSQO**—pronounced "cosh-coh"—is intoned once, followed by a deep in-breath and retention in which the medicine power of Mother Earth is drawn in through your *qosqo* and allowed to permeate your being. The practitioner then rotates clockwise one full circle, and the hands are moved into a position with thumbs touching, palms held parallel to the Earth at roughly waist level.
> **ALLPA**—pronounced "eye-pah"—is intoned once, followed by a deep in-breath and retention, incorporating the medicine power of the Earth element. The practitioner rotates clockwise one full circle. The hands are brought together in a cupped position at the level of the solar plexus.
> **UNU**—pronounced "ooo-nu"—is intoned once, followed by a deep in-breath and retention, incorporating the medicine power of the Water element. The practitioner rotates clockwise one full circle, and the hands are opened to the Heavens, palms at shoulder level.
> **WAYRA**—pronounced "why-rah"—is intoned once, followed by a deep in-breath and retention, incorporating the medicine power of the Air element. The practitioner rotates clockwise one full circle. The palms are extended forwards, perpendicular to the Earth, with elbows held at right angles.

NINA—pronounced "knee-nah"—is intoned once, followed by a deep in-breath and retention, incorporating the medicine power of the Fire element. The practitioner rotates clockwise one full circle. The thumbs and forefingers are again brought together to form a triangle, which is brought over the brow. With a wide stance, the back is arched to mimic the arc of the rainbow.

K'UYCHI—pronounced "coo-eee-chee"—is intoned once, followed by a deep in-breath and retention, incorporating the power of the luminous manifestation of the *T'eqse Muyu*. The practitioner rotates clockwise one full circle.

QOSQO—Once again, the *qosqo* hand position is assumed and QOSQO is intoned. The practitioner rotates clockwise one full circle. As the practitioner inhales, she opens her stance placing hands on the knees in a squatting style, as if giving birth. The breath is offered directly into the Earth.

Complete the full cycle three times. For enhanced spiritual alignment, complete this ritual once a day for one week. If possible, this is best done barefoot and outdoors.

The PRP is a yogic-like dance of the integrative, sacred relationship between five element-specific hand mudras, Quechua intonations, pranic breathing, postural positioning, and rotational spin. It represents becoming, merging, and being One with the living, pulsing, sacred matrix of Mother Earth. With consistent practice of the PRP, one eventually begins to experience its ritual enactment being consciously orchestrated by *Pachamama* herself, embodied as grace and flow.

GRATITUDE FUELS GENEROSITY WHICH OPENS TO GRACE

If the impulse of giving finds its roots in the ritual of ceremonial offering or giving thanks, it follows that love and fear are vital, driving forces behind the creative process. These emotions can become the inspiration of the shamanic healer in their intention to please the giver (either loved or feared) and the recipient (also either loved or feared). In other words, those creations cannot simply result from intellectual conceits. We can consider them more appropriately as conceived in the heart.

Throughout the entire shamanic arc of historical evolution, each time an offering is made to the spirit world, or to our tribal protector spirits or tutelary allies, it is received as love-sourced nourishment and spiritual sustenance to our tribal past. Every offering is a gift to our "protector," whether Divine or human. If we've put our hearts and souls into these ritual creations, this selfless generosity shall always be received as true art and good medicine. Therefore, we could say that both shamanic mastery and artistic brilliance proceed from the act of giving—from the Gift. For all art, whether in the form of shamanic ceremony, abstract-expressionist painting, or pre-Columbian textile weaving, is essentially a gift.

All human activity that matters to us and touches our heart, revives our soul, or offers courage for living, is received as Great Work and a sacred gift. All shamanic ceremony, every healing ritual, appeals to a part of our being which is itself a gift and not an acquisition.

In the ancient Andes, as in most ancient cultures, the shaman, the hierophant, or the priest king links the celestial to the terrestrial and the gods to man. This tradition has survived in many parts of the world and even in the most notable of modern religions, including Christianity with the Pope and Tibetan Buddhism with the Dalai Lama. For the ancient Andeans, the shaman and artist were one and the same, for the aim of both art and shamanism is transformation and elevation to another consciousness.

Part Three

The aim of the reverent practice of universal shamanism is beautifying the world through Earth-regenerative ceremonial artistry. The ritualist, as a visionary artist, simultaneously becomes a revealer of that which lies beyond what the eye perceives, and the mind can conceive. In other words, a shaman can become a "walker between worlds"—a supreme psychopomp—sharing stature with Persephone, Dante, Odysseus, Loki, Kukulkan, and your own immortal shamanic soul.

When performing artful rituals of reverence for Mother Nature befitting seven generations, the past becomes present. When heartfelt shamanic ceremonies are re-enacted at ancestrally venerated temple sites and pilgrimage destinations, we are joined in visionary intention and soul-restorative action with all adepts of the Great Work who have gone before us—our shamanic ancestors and their inner sources of healing power and spiritual wisdom. In fact, this contingent of seen and unseen Shining Ones has been showering blessings on our planet—through the intense force fields created by their spiritual practices— since time immemorial. I trust all people on our good Earth will tune in to these same graces. And hope it is sooner rather than later. So it is!

KEEPING THE FIRE ALIVE

Among the Inka of Peru there was a special class of cultural wisdom keepers known as the *Amauta*, whose duty it was to compose and perpetuate, from generation to generation, the traditions of the people by creating a history, legend and cosmovision. They were also given the task of preserving the rich storehouses of information about nature, humanity, and the balanced relationship of the two. This they inherited from their pre-Inka Chavin, Paracas, Nasca, Tiahuanaco, Moche, and Chimu predecessors. Any serious student of pre-Columbian culture would agree that the principal spiritual mission of indigenous Peruvian people is to create unity between nature and humankind.

Land, water, humanity, and cosmos are all exquisitely united in the *Amauta's* majestic temple sanctuaries, pilgrimage shrines, healing rituals, ceremonial practices, and societal norms. They serve the role as cultural repositories of their ancestors' ethno-spiritual vision and mythic oral traditions. By taking an oath to maintain this perennial cosmovision, undiluted in its essence, its healing practice is always guaranteed to point toward a renewal of creative powers and toward a condition that is vital, stirring, strong, and whole, as befits a creative original beginning.

Hence, a shaman in traditional tribal societies is often a major conservative force, preserving his or her culture and conserving the environment, particularly in the face of encroaching development and consumerism. An emerging form of global shamanistic traditions marks the expanded state of awareness and consciousness on the planet. This new model integrates old and multicultural traditions with new and future-based tools and techniques. Referred to as neo-shamanism or urban shamanism, this path is attuned to the wisdom and knowledge of ancient healing systems, modern medicine, and science, as well as new forms of healing and knowledge continuously being "discovered" today.

Even advanced science, engineering, and technology, though they are praised for their achievements, tend to be stifled by unresolvable paradoxes when they face the unseen. It is therefore not surprising that today's most celebrated popularizers of cutting-edge discoveries in cosmology and quantum physics, have sought answers from perennial wisdom traditions and ancient spiritual texts that support the existence of an invisible, preternatural causative force responsible for creation.

It is even less surprising that millions of post-modern women, men, and children find existential refuge and life purpose from the shamanic legacy of our original peoples. As a universal path of spirit-informed healing and life, and of regenerative communion with nature and creation, shamanism is also the foundation of its own rebirth and its increasingly widespread global appeal. Because it is such an enduring healing vocation and spiritual avocation, we may confidently say that universal shamanism is here to stay.

A JOURNEY THROUGH THE ANCIENT PRESENT

Let's pretend for just a moment that we are on an ancient journey. We are a nomadic, Earth-honoring clan of multicultural shamanic healers, wisdom keepers, storytellers, singers, dancers, and seasoned ceremonialists. We are an ancestral, star-seeded family of gnostic adepts long initiated into the Great Work. We are all passionate about our shamanic prowess in beautifying and sanctifying our species-wide life upon beloved *Pachamama*. We are a rainbow tribe of soul-awakened Gaian passersby traveling through distant lands in centuries past. We freely and fearlessly have embarked on a spiritually motivated walkabout—a flawlessly preordained visionary sojourn of light, love, and deep listening.

We pilgrimage to destinations of unimaginable beauty, each place punctuated by stunning examples of human ingenuity. We visit breathtaking megalithic temples, ancestrally venerated ceremonial sites, and legendary sacred power places. We live the mythic tales and tribal legends of days gone by. We experience the epic narratives and hear the great fables and origin stories of cultures long departed. We see the teachings of enlightened ones down through the ages.

What do the ancient myths tell us? What messages do these great teachers have to share with us modern-day travelers?

Our ears and our eyes open. We hear cries of anguish. We see tears shed by men and women of all nationalities, gentle souls who wanted nothing more than peace in their lives. We hear their pleas for justice. We hear their soft voices speaking of a better day to come. We see unnecessary suffering inflicted on people by other people. We see brutality. We see torture. We feel the sadness of children denied a loving hand. We know this pain and misery continue, year after year, generation after generation. We see as much as our hearts and souls can bear. And yet, through it all, we see smiles and laughter. Ironically, we hear the continuous sound of celebration. We see the faces of wise ones glowing with joy. Invariably, they speak of hope. Their message is clear. They talk to us with certainty, for they know that life is a Game— *Pukllay Kawsay.*

Part Three

We acknowledge that the heart yearns for wholeness and love while the mind craves control and approval. We recognize that solutions based on work and struggle are contrived by the mind. Political, legislative, and overfunded organizational strategies to resolve our world's problems are all generated and carried out by undisciplined, ego-driven minds. These strategies cannot result in fundamental change. Looking at history, we see they have not.

Since a solely mind-oriented way of approaching a situation clouds the truth, such methods can only worsen things. A natural solution, a true and lasting resolution of our planetary crisis, must come from the heart. The heart must be our source of inspired guidance. We require a different approach.

The enlightened ones of long ago foresaw our current world crisis. Their legends are full of accounts that foretold our world today. These ancient teachers knew the dangers we would face. They spoke to us repeatedly about what to do. They said compassionate acceptance and the way of the heart would be the way forward. They explained the futility of denial and fear. Through the ages, these wise souls have dropped countless hints on how to best play the game. We graciously accept their generous offerings and apply them whenever we can.

History shows us that where there is no vision, the people perish. Well, we are the vision, and we have a game plan. By accepting current reality, while— at the same time—focusing on our visionary purpose of attaining global unity, we will transform planetary consciousness and shift human destiny from material breakdown to spiritual breakthrough. The central action of this approach is acceptance, not denial. Painful as it is, dismal as it looks, hopeless as it feels, we must nonetheless recognize and wholeheartedly embrace a spirit-informed shamanic approach in our acceptance of current reality. Doing so, while maintaining our life-affirming vision, is the essence of *Pukllay Kawsay*.

Gaia-*Pachamama*, our beloved Mother Earth, experienced tremendous geophysical upheavals, species-wide biological transformations, and many other dramatic, planetary metamorphoses eons before she could support life as we know it. Science acknowledges that human activity is putting *Pachamama's* ability to support abundant human life in peril. Many indigenous stories talk about the harm and suffering caused by humankind's voluntary separation from what gives us life.

Still, we have the know-how and practices that can help restore sanity and balance. As we teach love by how we live, we send forth responsive evolutionary consciousness in healing service for our seven generations and beyond.

The energy surrounding and permeating our planet is filled and transformed by a higher vibration of love and connection that positively impacts health, healing, and relationships. The allure of excessive materiality is powerful, and world economies depend upon consumption to keep the status quo afloat. It's quite a precarious situation and a dangerous game, one opposite the perennial wisdom teachings of *Pukllay Kawsay*—the Game of Life.

TAKING IT TO THE STREETS

As humans, we have been given a reflective consciousness and a capacity to witness the flow of life beyond the perimeters of the self. We know of life's needs and preoccupations. This capacity is so much more than an intellectual capacity to reason, analyze problems, and predict consequences. It is the compassionate capacity to feel the resonance of the wider universe, a more inclusive world, and to experience a deep reverence for all life.

Our ability to develop inclusive compassion is greater now than ever. Of course, we have far to go, but we see inspired global responses to natural catastrophes and epidemic diseases; we see a rise in philanthropic ventures. We see thousands of organizations promoting human rights, social justice, poverty alleviation, species-wide restorative ecology, and the widespread honoring and celebration of traditional native arts and aboriginal culture. Yet only a handful of people are seriously focused on the preservation and contemporary revitalization of endangered shamanic wisdom traditions.

It is no secret that the diversity of indigenous cultures around the world is increasingly threatened due to the use of political violence, forced resettlement, and the pressure to assimilate. As pioneers of universal shamanism in the post-modern world, we must focus on bringing together worldwide native leaders and pro-indigenous activist organizations dedicated to addressing human rights violations, assisting tribal communities to reclaim and manage their ancestral lands, and offer them support in determining their own future. We must address the need to develop social and economic empowerment tools that support indigenous efforts to effectively resist cultural degradation and threats to their sovereignty.

For those of us initiated into universal shamanism, our vision is guided by a cross-cultural shamanic focus on the importance of incorporating ancestral indigenous traditions within the world at large. We offer these traditions to share; not to risk becoming polarized by political issues, but to show what it means to be a unified global family.

To bring worldwide attention to the critical challenges facing most original peoples of our planet, we must first bring the ancestral wisdom traditions—such as Earth-honoring ceremonies and shamanic healing practices—of indigenous peoples into the modern Western world. Until we include the ethno-spiritual wisdom of our ancestral peoples in the dominant global institutions responsible for the social and economic well-being of humanity, we shall continue our downward spiral and become increasingly estranged from the sacred dimensions of life.

As Earth-honoring practitioners of universal shamanism, we are in a privileged position to offer visionary guidance and pragmatic, Earth-honoring solutions to our modern technological society. To ensure such a benevolent transformational influence upon our global community, I offer the following Seven Lessons as a cross-cultural shamanic protocol by which to guide our ethno-spiritual activism:

Lesson Number 1

You can't compel other people to change their consciousness in a particular direction; you can simply make it easier.

Lesson Number 2

People don't get moved through being persuaded. People get moved through being aligned.

Lesson Number 3

You can't get a group to work together successfully without first taking care of their hearts and souls.

Lesson Number 4

Help others enter communion with the natural world, because the experience of reconnection with the living Earth arouses desire to act on its behalf.

Lesson Number 5

Acting on behalf of something greater than yourself leads to a feeling that something is acting through you with a greater power than your own.

Lesson Number 6

Through group, ritual participation, the past becomes present. Through universal shamanic ceremonial practice, when performed in the proper and customary manner, the present participants are linked to all those who have gone before. The ceremony links us to the shamanic ancestors and their inner sources of healing power and spiritual wisdom. Great souls are constantly showering blessings on the planet through the intense force fields created by their spiritual practices. Tune in!

Lesson Number 7
You do not need to see the results of your work. When we remain non-attached to the outcome of our individual and collective efforts, we greatly increase our chance of being pleasantly surprised in the long run.

In essence, the ideal way to mainstream the Universal Shamanism way of life within our modern, technological society is by living a life that exemplifies the above seven lessons as a cross-cultural, shamanic path dedicated to the spiritual reawakening of humanity. The ceremonial mastery involved in Universal Shamanism focuses on harnessing deeply transformative forces and spiritual powers for the healing of our world. I therefore appeal to all the pro-indigenous organizations and respected advocates of aboriginal rights to embody this all-inclusive, visionary approach of giving expression to the ancient voices of our original peoples—with brothers and sisters from all nations, races, and walks of life—as we sojourn together into the third millennium.

REFLECTIONS ON OUR PLANETARY RITE OF PASSAGE

Pachakuti is an ancestral Inka wisdom precept that speaks to life's inherent, cyclical nature involving periods of creation, preservation, and the destruction of a species or environmental habitat. The word means "world reversal" or "cosmic transformation." A *Pachakuti* is the ritual transmogrification of chaos into order and breakdown into a breakthrough. From the perspective of Andean shamanic traditions, the whole-systems crisis experienced on Earth offers us a unique evolutionary opportunity to midwife a new way of being human that transcends the polarizing ideological origins behind our current Great Turning.

Evolution is punctuated by the sudden, unforeseen appearances of novel forms of life. We can expect the same from humankind's soul maturation and psycho-spiritual growth. Answers about death and afterlife work on probabilities. Even catastrophe is conditional. Ultimately, it is our job to show up, be fully present, and speak our truth, unencumbered by fear, doubt, or insecurity. We are asked to give empathic flight to our hearts and free our minds from the constraints of scientific materialism and religious fundamentalism.

The time is now, and now is the time! We are experiencing the "perfect storm," the ideal moment for allowing our soul-awakened imagination of what is possible to soar upon the wings of condor and eagle. Our creative partnership with the sacred, spiral imprint of evolution is vital if we are to gracefully align our experience of unity consciousness with life's wonderfully unpredictable nature and the intrinsic, regenerative power of transformation, flow, and change. Now is the perfect time for discovery and growth.

In a spirit of playful, childlike creativity, wonderment, and awe—with curiosity, inventiveness, and dreams—we are invited to sing and dance our seven-generation service vision into the world as a labor of love. The long-prophesied evolutionary process orchestrating our human re-membering as a life-affirming and Spirit-imbued presence on the planet, first and foremost, requires a radical surrender of all craving for approval and control.

Only then shall we be able to selflessly harness the Great Originating Mystery's wisdom to serve as our beneficent transformational healing light for the world. As *Pachamama's* beloved children, empowered by a shared experience of reverence for All Our Relations, we shall again walk in beauty upon Gaia's hallowed ground. Remember this. Experience it. Be it. *Hinayá!*

A PATH OF PEACEFUL LIVING

Peace, tranquility, ease, calm, repose, serenity, stillness, equanimity, and bliss are a few other words used to describe what ancestral Quechua speaking peoples of Peru experience as *Oasi-kawsay*, or "peace" in the Quechua language of the Andes. It is understood as a lived experience, an emergent process, intrinsic to human nature, a surrendered flow into being at one with the dance of creation, a merging with the ebb and flow of life itself. Never static, it is encountered, like a bestowal of grace it is a 'touching into' the pause between activity and rest . . . requiring us to remain experientially connected to the ever-changing liminal dreaming between sky and earth, self and other, heart and mind, soul, and body.

Among the contemporary descendants of the Inka, there still exists a special class of wisdom keeper, the *Qasi-kawsay Yachachiq* or "teacher of peace," whose duty, as dharma, is to compose and perpetuate from generation to generation the embodiment of serene living born of *munay*, best described as compassionate feeling and unlimited love. Teaching this Divine expression of love by the way they live, is known to awaken in others the experience of *munay* as a human birthright.

I thus invite you to join me on a journey of watching quietly and anticipating nothing, of remaining open to all that is here and now, looking deeply into yourself while reading these words. Read them slowly as you feel the way you are sitting, sensing your body, conscious of a co-arising in the movement of thought and feeling, and the way your breath comes and goes— being a witness and the witnessed, passively watching and actively being watched. You are now fully attentive that there can be a further letting go, a beginning relationship to an unchanging inner stillness—open, in reverence, to a re-membering of Self as a luminous strand within the Great Sacred Web of Life we lovingly call *Gaia-Pachamama*. This, my beloveds, is the lived experience of *Qasi-kawsay* embraced by the ancestral shamanic lineages of the Andes.

May this offering of word and practice find receptivity in your hearts as a healing catalyst for the blossoming of global peace within our lives.

THE ONLY WAY OUT IS WITHIN

There has never been a greater need for the soul-vivifying beauty ways of our shamanic ancestors. The often-quoted Hopi adage, "We are the ones we've been waiting for," clearly epitomizes the wisdom that when united we are naturally endowed with the imaginative and physical resources for positively impacting even the most challenging of life's vicissitudes. Long prophesied by our Amerindian original people humankind stands at a new beginning. We've been gifted a dream of a historical interlude for evolving beyond our survival based individual obsessions. We are being called into a recollecting of ourselves as a unified and spiritually awakened force for good in the world. What lies ahead for humanity is not a research project, nor a question hoping for an answer. Instead, it is simply an evolutionary process, a natural unfolding and flow of our Divine essence at this exact time, a flow that begins with our first breath and may not end with our last.

As humans we are inextricably bound to an ongoing river through which flows the emergence of a universal sentience that has no name. Even so we persist in naming: Spirit, Source, Tao, God, Yahweh, Allah, *Wakan Tanka, Hunab Ku, T'eqse Muyu,* Creator, Creatrix, Great Originating Mystery, and most recently, the Higgs-boson Source Code. In the flow, merry or not merry, we meet and part and meet again. Yet our meetings are potent, vital, stirring, and can be life aligning, profoundly uplifting, and bounteous for our lives, like any new happening has the potential to be. I believe it was Rupert Sheldrake whom I once heard say: "The way we envision the world can restore its soul, and the way in which the world is ensouled can restore our vision."

Quite sage advice for a world so desperately in need of experiencing the primacy of consciousness—that is, the presence of soul in things material. We have models for this, ancient and new. An exquisite example is the ancient Hindu conceptualization of Indra's Web—best described as an innately conscious self-reflexive multidimensional matrix—a Divinely interconnected network—in which each point of meeting, of joining, is a spherical jewel much like a pearl. Each radiantly rounded gem reflects all others, a holographic mirroring of infinitude, all things vibrating in resonance with all others, a living nexus of non-linear dynamics, a "cloud of points" as posited by Nobel Laureate physicist Ilya Prigogine. More recently, research in a field called Complexity Theory has illumined the capacity of bees, termites, ants, and even humans to instinctively yield collective wisdom and adaptive sustenance together, in resonance with each other, which they are not able to hold in their individual beings, when separate from the whole.

So, my question is: What might you be holding, that I might be holding, that we cannot manifest in our separate selves, but may find together in a hive of process? Is this not what these times are calling us to do? These troubled, uncertain, dangerous, wildly transformative, wonderfully unpredictable powerful times? Is it not the time to get to the heart, and most importantly the soul, of what it means to be a planetary human species here and now? Can we provide an antidote to the modern stigmata of feeling we are "not enough" that is too often sought alleviation with "too-muchness"—more stuff, more money, more Santa's elves hyping disposable trinkets? Can we once again feel the natural turning of the earth, the seasons, and the essential Divinity within our existence? Will humanity be generative, hopeful, and learn to blissfully embrace mystery and all things Ineffable as in times past? I say *yes*, we absolutely can!

For such a heroic undertaking, we must first reclaim the courage, vision, and the will to delve down into the alchemical depths of our soul. We must fully accept the immortal sovereignty of our universal Self and learn to lovingly dwell in *Śūnyatā*, or "primordial empty fullness"—an Empyrean realm of omniscience where our consciousness and Ultimate Ground of Being become indistinguishable. It is through such experience of Divine embrace that we shall rediscover the experience of reverence and loving grace that sparked the emergence of shamanism as a universal path of healing service for our world.

BECOMING ONE IN THE GARDEN

Thus, we re-member, once again, through our memory of the Original Oath, first spoken, then summoned, as we became one in the garden. May this be heard by all those in heaven and earth, donning ears that yield subtle celestial resonances, souls able to embrace a purposeful life mirrored in creation, eternally free of the fears and limitations of long-ago disillusionment. To such souls, I have been sanctioned to write these words.

For those who have mastered the harmonics that praise the music of the spheres, that are moved by sweetly betrothed Divine whisperings, the graces of truth revealed when listened through the heart, they will hear with their gift of faith made flesh. A promising vision of light, love, and healing born from Above, I have been asked to bequeath Below. And here we stand together, trusted children of Mother Earth, in another time and another place, again offered the beauty, bounty, and blessing of becoming one in the garden. The choice is ours.

Eternal blessings on your universal shamanic beauty walk, cherished friends—see you in cosmic dream time!

Sonqoymanta (with heart),
don Oscar

APPENDIX

*A Celebration of Our
Shamanic Animal Allies*

Shamanic animal allies—also known as spirit helpers, tutelary animals, totemic powers, and guardian spirits—are integral to a shaman's work. In traditional shamanic societies, the more animal spirits a tribal shaman had under their mandate, the more influential and powerful they were. Whether they were encountered during magical flight in search of a person's wayward soul or met when on pilgrimage to some ancestral destination, animals have been critical companions in assisting the shaman accomplish the task at hand.

Tribal shamans view chance meetings with animals as sources of great power and creative energy that protect, sustain, and guide them in their own lives and in working with others. Shamans consider it a profound honor and privilege to be identified with a particular animal as the source of one's shamanic healing power. Totemic animal allies are present among shamanic peoples the world over.

Although today's world might be vastly different from that of our shamanic ancestors, we have access to the same powerful guidance for healing and navigating difficult situations. Mother Nature often finds ways of reminding us we are not alone, including our through fortuitous encounters with our animal relatives. Whether observing the majestic flight of a condor circling above glacial mountain peaks or noticing the persistent image of a mountain lion on a billboard, animals can be considered "signs" of a user-friendly, shamanic universe conspiring to support us.

RITUAL PROCESS

To effectively manifest the full healing virtue and guidance associated with any of the five groupings of shamanic animal allies featured below, you must first call upon the fullness of that animal ally's medicine soul in service to your shamanic path. To do so, you'll need to carve out between fifteen and twenty minutes of uninterrupted, personal space-time and wholeheartedly summon, align, and merge with your chosen animal's medicine beauty. You can fully awaken in consciousness and viscerally activate any chosen animal ally's medicine beauty in the following ways:

1. Have available a printed copy of your chosen animal's ritual invocation.
2. Temporarily put aside all other worldly obligations and responsibilities.
3. Choose or create a peaceful and, ideally, uncluttered indoor or outdoor space to properly honor this simple ritual practice. Feel free to use incense, sage, aromatic waters, music, a small altar, or anything else you feel would further sanctify your ritual space.
4. Once comfortably seated, with eyes closed and body relaxed, spend two to three minutes engaged in slow, deep, lower diaphragmatic breathing through the nose.
5. Silently read the printed copy of the ritual invocation, fully absorbing its wisdom in heart and mind.
6. After a brief, contemplative silence, read the entire invocation aloud. Feel your chosen animal's medicine soul energetically in your solar plexus.
7. Place your printed copy in front of you. Close your eyes and blissfully surrender into whatever you feel in your body or consciousness.
8. Ideally, perform this ritual once a day for seven consecutive days, preferably at the same time each day.

Note: If you are concerned about properly pronouncing the Quechua words interspersed within the invocations, please simply cross or blank them out.

The same soul-empowered, shamanic medicine is available to you when reading the invocation with or without the Quechua terms. Remember, dear ones, developing competency as a shamanic practitioner relies on our purity of motive and clarity of intention as ritualists.

THE FIVE PRINCIPAL ANIMAL ALLIES OF UNIVERSAL SHAMANISM

AMARU

Related totem: Boa, anaconda, and all other types of creepy crawlers and slithering relatives
Associated medicine virtue: *Kawsay*—The vital life force used to heal bodily conditions and transform material life circumstances.
Associated element: *Allpa*—Earth
Human attribute: *Llankay*—Right action, meaningful work, industriousness

Amaru is a powerful animal that obtains its prey and moves across the earth and through the forest canopy with the incredible strength of its physical body. For this reason, *Amaru* is a powerful totem of the physical plane. A true representative of life and transformation, *Amaru* sheds what no longer serves it so that it can grow. *Amaru* is also an ally, throughout the world, to healers and masters of the earthly realm. This beautiful and powerful being brings you deep into your senses and reminds you that gaining mastery requires hard work.

As the tutelary spirit—a guardian or protector—of the south/southeast direction within your consecrated ceremonial space, *Amaru* represents the earth element. Earth grounds us to that which is tangible and is the source and end place of our bodies. It is both the cradle and the grave. This polarity can invite you to investigate the polarities of the positive and the perceived negative aspects in yourself. The earth element speaks to befriending those so-called "negative" aspects so you can stand confidently in truth within this dimension.

Amaru is a superb animal ally to call upon if you are suffering from physical imbalances such as fatigue, sluggishness, lack of motivation, laziness, or overall bodily weakness caused by biological infirmity. At the other end of the physical polarity, the spontaneous and frequent appearance of *Amaru* in dreams or shamanic journeywork usually indicates an overly hedonistic and/or materialistic perspective on life. Because *Amaru* is a totem of transformation, it can also be a great ally if you are feeling stuck, resigned, or disconnected from your soul's innate need for communion with *Mamapacha*—Mother Nature.

If *Amaru* has become a frequent totemic visitor and companion in your life—that is, often showing up in either physical or imaginal form as boa, anaconda, or any other type of creepy crawling and slithering relative—it is important to assess how you are earning your right livelihood, growing, and transforming. Are you choosing to physically express yourself by working too much or too little? Should you care for your physical body better, so that you can make your dreams a reality? Or perhaps you are too focused on work or the physical and need to find balance. What do you need to shed so you can grow?

If you are fearful of snakes, perhaps you might ask yourself if hard work or other physical elements of your world are dominating you or creating fear or blockages in your life. Sit with this fear and allow it to inform you. If you are not already doing so, keep a daily journal in which to write or illustrate any significant epiphanies or insights you receive as you engage this deeper level of self-discovery. *Amaru* will always illuminate a path of meaningful work and Earth-centered right action in the world.

A RITUAL INVOCATION TO *AMARU*

Praises to *Hatun Amaru*, great boa and anaconda animal ally; Divine child of *Pachamama*, the earth mother; sacred guardian of south and southeast directions; noble shamanic gatekeeper of the *Qollasuyu*; elemental embodiment of *Allpa*; sacred earth, formed as stone; supreme healer of physical infirmity and harmonizer of material dissonance. Come in, medicine beauty of *Amarupa Hampin Munaycha*, Divine serpent spirit presence born of creation's love, *Sonqoypi Tupakuy Kawsaypi Qhawakuy*. Meet yourself in my heart, see yourself in my life. Sustainer of illumined sensing, bestower of healthful balance for our bodies, wisdom tutelary of *Llankay*, right action as an awakened vocation. Master teacher of conscious independence in healing service to self, I invoke your gift of intrapersonal awareness… I evoke my medicine virtue as shaman and healer, empowered by *Kawsay*… I thus decree myself in purpose as a catalyst and sustainer of personal evolution within the life of humankind—*Hinaya!*

CHALLWA

Related totem: Dolphin, whale, and all other types of swimmers and aquatic relatives
Associated medicine virtue: *Samisonqoy*—The heart-animating essence. Used to heal emotional or affective conditions and transform dysfunctional interpersonal relationships.
Associated element: *Unu*—Water
Human attribute: *Munay*—Unlimited love, compassionate feeling, altruistic caring

Appendix

Challwa are social and communicative with a deep connection to the emotional body. Your companions of the sea are here to remind you to be playful, to speak with an open heart, and to connect with your family, friends, and community so that you, and they, receive deep blessings. A Challwa encounter inspires awe, magic, and an expansive sense of joy and playfulness. Your heart is at the core of your being and the center of your life. Heart connections with others bring your greatest joy and deepest pain. Let Challwa be your guide as you journey into your heart so you can feel the joy, connection, compassion, and freedom that is your birthright.

The Challwa is your messenger and speaks to you through the emotional element of water. Water is the source of all life and the home of *Munay*—unlimited and unconditional love. Let your dolphin support you in touching the depth of your feelings so that you can help face, embrace, and compassionately navigate the complex and beautiful world of emotions, to benefit yourself and others.

The Challwa can be a particularly good ally for you in areas of your life and your relationships where you feel disharmony or stress between you and others. If you are feeling depressed, numb, broken-hearted, isolated, disconnected, or alone, Challwa medicine can help you align with what you need to help guide you back home.

Challwa medicine can also illuminate the higher knowing of your emotions. When you invite the presence of Challwa, you will be given support to seek out the company of loved ones and become more present to the company you keep. The Challwa invites you to ask: Are you in need of reconnection or more time with friends or family members? Have you been shutting someone out of your life that you should be letting in? Are you keeping company that frazzles, devalues, or drains you? Challwa will guide you to trust what you are feeling emotionally and to find the harmony you seek. Challwa as a guide can also remind you to play, dance, have child-like fun, and take the events of your life a little less seriously. Water might also be powerful healing medicine to you now. Perhaps a playful swim in a river, lake, or the ocean—or a hot bath—is just what you need.

A RITUAL INVOCATION TO CHALLWA

Praises to *Hatun Challwa*, great dolphin or whale animal ally, Divine child of *Mama Killa*, mother moon, sacred guardian of west and southwest directions, noble shamanic gatekeeper of the *Kuntisuyu*. Elemental embodiment of *Unu*, sacred water, formed as shell, supreme healer of emotional infirmity: Come in medicine beauty of *Challwapa Hampin Munaycha*, Divine swimmer and spirit presence, born of Creation's love. *Sonqoypi Tupakuy Kawsaypi Qhawakuy*, meet yourself in my heart, see yourself in my life. Sustainer of illumined feeling, bestower of healthful balance for our hearts, wisdom tutelary of *Munay*, unlimited compassionate love as awakened caring. Master teacher of conscious dependence in healing service to others, I invoke your gift of interpersonal awareness… I evoke my medicine virtue as artist and ritualist, empowered by *Samisonqoy*. I thus decree myself in purpose as catalyst and sustainer of communal evolution within the life of humankind—*Hinaya!*

KUNTUR

Related totem: Condor, eagle, hawk, hummingbird, and other types of winged and sky-oriented relatives

Associated medicine virtue: *K'anchay*—Spiritual light energy used for healing conditions of disconnection from source and transforming constricted transpersonal relationships with the Divine.

Associated element: *Wayra*—Air

Human attribute: *Yuyay*—Disembodied spirit awareness, remembering, higher intuition

Appendix

Kunturs fly high in the sky, so they have a vast perspective across the land. They have always been known as important messengers of spirit and gatekeepers between humans and the world of mystery. In fact, it is believed that the white collars donned by priests were originally inspired by the white collar of the spiritually aligned Kuntur. Our winged relatives connect us to Spirit, to our intuition, and to the big picture. When your earthwork can be guided by the presence of Spirit and the clear vision of Kuntur, you will naturally be drawn into a deeper alignment with your intuition, or spiritual intelligence, which will be available to serve not only you, but all beings. It will then be easier to live in the awareness that we are one human family, descended from stardust.

To see a bird as magnificent as the great Kuntur is a moment one does not easily forget. In fact, an encounter with any large raptor makes us draw breath deep into our bodies and wonder about what's possible. There is a truth beyond all truths that we hold inside of each of us. Let Kuntur's clear vision and presence of spirit draw you into a deeper alignment with your intuition.

Kuntur speaks to you through the element of air. Air is the birthplace of the Great Originating Mystery and the element of spiritual remembering, intuition, and pure possibility. It is also the place where communication is born. Air highlights the importance of the things that you say and how you listen and dialogue with others.

The condor can be a particularly good ally for you if you are suffering from disharmony in the spiritual or transcendental realm. Perhaps you are feeling lost or disconnected, or maybe a vague dis-ease or aimlessness is eating at you. Or you have an inability to trust your intuition, or a fear of taking the leap toward what you know you must do.

Kuntur medicine will illuminate the Divine knowing within you so that you may learn to trust it once again. When inviting the presence of Kuntur, you will be given support to follow the subtle—and not-so-subtle—

invitations from Spirit so that you can be of best service. Is your gut telling you something that you have been ignoring? Have you been checking in with your intuition at all? Or, if you have, have you been unable to take the next step into what you know you must do?

If Kuntur has come into your life, consider the impact of communication in your life. Have you been communicating clearly and authentically from your heart in the ways you should be? Have you been listening and offering those important to you the opportunity for dialogue?

Air medicine can be a powerful force for those who are inviting in Kuntur. You may want to look for ways to reap its benefits. Maybe a visit to a beach or hilltop where you can feel the breeze, or a breathwork practice such as *pranayama*, would be of service to you. Kuntur reminds you that you are a palette for the Divine impulse of creation. The more you open the channels to that impulse in your life, the more beauty, truth, and goodness is possible in the world.

A RITUAL INVOCATION TO KUNTUR

Praises to *Hatun Kuntur*, great condor or eagle animal ally, Divine child of *Wiracocha*, creator/creatrix of our Great Originating Mystery, sacred guardian of north and northwest directions, noble shamanic gatekeeper of the *Chinchaysuyu*. Elemental embodiment of *Wayra*, sacred air, formed as feather, supreme healer of spiritual infirmity. Come in, medicine beauty of *Kunturpa Hampin Munaycha*, Divine winged spirit presence born of Creation's love, *Sonqoypi Tupakuy Kawsaypi Qhawakuy*, meet yourself in my heart and see yourself in my life. Sustainer of illumined intuiting, bestower of healthful balance for our spirit, wisdom tutelary of *Yuyay*, transcendent awareness and spiritual remembering through awakened vision. Master teacher of conscious interdependence in healing service to the world, I invoke your gift of transpersonal awareness. I evoke my medicine virtue as visionary and seer, empowered by *K'anchay*. I thus decree myself in purpose as catalyst and sustainer of planetary evolution within the life of humankind—*Hinaya!*

POMA

Related totem: Puma, jaguar, and all other four-legged, mammalian-type relatives

Associated medicine virtue: *Samiumay*—Mind-animating essence used to heal mental and psychological conditions and transform disturbances of an intrapersonal nature related to our human psyche.

Associated element: *Nina*—Fire

Human attribute: *Yachay*—Wisdom, higher intelligence

If you encounter a Poma or other large cat, a sense of regal reverence may invite your body into a poised and relaxed state. The order and direction of your life can be so much bigger than you dare to dream. Let Poma be your guide as you journey into your higher mind to discover the universal awareness and wisdom that is the key to your true purpose and destiny.

The graceful, strong, and elusive big cats are powerful totems, and Poma is no exception. Pomas have a powerful presence of respect and surrender. Beyond all else, they possess a razor-sharp insight and awareness. That is why Poma is an ally of the mind and the psychic plane and is a messenger that can awaken you to the awareness of the vast and incredible power of the great universal wisdom. Poma is the guide that reminds you of the adage, "The mind is a wonderful servant but a terrible master." Because of its ability to see beyond ordinary perception, Poma has a knack for illuminating right order in your life and reminding you that your thoughts are destined to become tangible things in this world.

Poma is a totem of the east, the direction of the sun—*Inti*. Poma as a guide may speak to you through the sun or fire. In its highest form, the Poma represents the brilliant and illuminating servant of creation.

Poma can be a particularly good ally for you if you are experiencing disharmony in your mind and thoughts. If you are suffering from anxiety, over-judgment, confusion, control issues, or are feeling like you are overanalyzing and stuck in the cogs of your own mind, Poma medicine may be just what you need to detach yourself and remember a higher truth.

The medicine beauty of the Poma can illuminate the importance of universal remembrance and support you in surrendering yourself to a higher order. When inviting the presence of Poma, you will be given support to head in the right direction and take the steps needed to move toward your highest destiny. Are you seeing the big picture in your life? Is there any way for you to pan out and connect with the greater order? What is the next step you need to take to pursue the highest order of things? Poma can support you with these questions. If Poma has come into your life, the sun or element of fire may also be powerful medicine to you. In what ways can you honor the energies or gifts of the sun? Perhaps some time spent sunbathing, hiking on a sunny afternoon, or sitting by the fire might assist you in receiving the blessings you need.

A RITUAL INVOCATION TO POMA

Praises to *Hatun Poma*, great poma or jaguar animal ally, Divine child of *Tayta Inti*, Father Sun, sacred guardian of east and northeast directions, noble shamanic gatekeeper of the *Antisuyu*. Elemental embodiment of *Nina*, sacred fire, formed as flamed candle, supreme healer of mental infirmity. Come in medicine beauty of *Pomapa Hampin Munaycha*, Divine, four-legged spirit presence born of Creation's love. *Sonqoypi Tupakuy Kawsaypi Qhawakuy*, meet yourself in my heart, see yourself in my life. Sustainer of illumined thinking, bestower of healthful balance for our minds, wisdom tutelary of *Yachay*, enlightened wisdom and higher intelligence through awakened cognition. Master teacher of conscious transcendence in healing service to the cosmos, I invoke your gift of universal awareness… I evoke my medicine virtue as teacher and sage, empowered by *Samiumay*… I thus decree myself in purpose as catalyst and sustainer of galactic evolution within the life of humankind—*Hinaya!*

LLAMA

Related totem: Alpaca, guanaco, vicuña, and other camelid-type relatives
Associated medicine virtue: *Illanunay*—Soul radiance used for healing conditions of estrangement from life's sacred dimensions and transforming fragmented experiences of wholeness.
Associated element: *T'eqsekallpa*—Aether
Human attribute: *Huñuy*—To unite, make whole, complete

If you see a Llama, you may find a sense of easy joy and comfort starts to become more accessible. This is partly because they embody the truth that we are all a part of one fabric, the great whole, common in our own uniqueness. Let Llama be your guide on the journey to remembering your wholeness and to integrating with the great cosmic force that is everything.

Llama is a guardian of the fifth element, the sacred rainbow. The sacred rainbow represents our common uniqueness and our integration as one with the universe. It reminds us that we are a woven rainbow sewn into the fabric of everything.

Llama represents the power to heal and harmonize disturbances of the soul or etheric plane. Llama is an excellent ally if you are feeling divided, compartmentalized, or like you can't really be yourself. A common issue that Llama helps to address is the feeling that you must keep your spiritual life separate from your professional or personal lives. Division in this way damages soul expression in all areas of life.

Llama as a guide illuminates your wholeness and reminds you that you are already beautiful and complete. It can be helpful to think about this message in your life as existing inside the center of a wheel. If you stray out from the center onto any spoke in the wheel, the ride will become increasingly bumpy and chaotic. Any part of your life in which you might become separated from wholeness will have a similar effect.

If Llama comes into your life, this ally may be telling you to pull back from anything you might be over-invested in at the cost of wholeness. Are you throwing away the baby with the bathwater? Is the ride of your life feeling bumpy and chaotic? Perhaps you must find a way down the spoke and back to the center of the wheel to ground in the truth of who you are. If Llama comes into your life, you may want to connect to the sacred rainbow element by eliciting joyfulness. Perhaps just watching a funny movie, doing something playful, and not taking yourself so seriously will be the right medicine, helping you to come back to your center. Llama wants you to remember that we live in a benevolent universe, willing and waiting to serve us, should we choose to allow it. You are already a part of it.

A RITUAL INVOCATION TO LLAMA

Praises to *Hatun Llama*, great llama or alpaca animal ally, Divine child of *Sumaq K'uychi*, supreme rainbow, sacred guardian of the center and middle directions, noble shamanic gatekeeper of the *Chawpinsuyu*. Elemental embodiment of *T'eqse Kallpa*, sacred aether formed as central shamanic power object, supreme healer of soul infirmity. Come in, medicine beauty of *Llamapa Hampin Munaycha*, Divine camelid spirit-presence born of Creation's love. *Sonqoypi Tupakuy Kawsaypi Qhawakuy*, meet yourself in my heart, see yourself in my life. Sustainer of illumined presence, bestower of healthful balance for our soul, wisdom tutelary of *Huñuy*, unified being and wholeness through awakened presence. Master teacher of conscious immanence in healing service to Creation, I invoke your gift of impersonal awareness... I evoke my medicine virtue as mystic and hierophant, empowered by *Illanunay*... I thus decree myself in purpose as catalyst and sustainer of multidimensional evolution within the life of humankind—*Hinaya!*

MEET OUR SACRED STORYTELLERS

ANNETTE ASSMY is a filmmaker, creative soul, mistress of ceremonies, and she is walking the path of an earth keeper. For her it is a heart wish to bring the soul nourishing Inca wisdom to the western world. She is the founder of the Mystery School of the Soul which launched in 2021. mysteryschoolofthesoul.com and chaskawisdom.com.

ARMINE BONN was born in Stuttgart, Germany, in 1958. After graduation she worked in the Department of Education. Armine has lived in North America, Mexico, Costa Rica, and China.

DIANE E. BROITMAN has lived almost fifty years on her path and received many gifts from the kingdom within. She now shares her wisdom with whomever feels called to live from their Higher Self.

NANCY E. BROWN was born in Montana where she met her first star beings at the age of three years old. Currently residing in British Columbia, she lives her life in ceremony.

WILLIAM O. FOGARTY is a non-binary practitioner of cross-cultural shamanism of the Pachakuti Mesa Tradition, as well as a facilitator of creative-wellbeing, creative process, and other integrative wellness experiences. clifecreativity.com.

RODNEY GARCIA, M.D. is a medical doctor and practitioner of the Pachakuti Mesa Tradition of cross-cultural shamanism. His work outside of the allopathic settings is founded in traditional Peruvian medicine of the Highlands and Amazonian regions, as well as incorporating traditional North American and Meso-American practices. taripaypacha-us.com.

YSETTE ROCES GUEVARA, PH.D. gardens in co-creative partnership with nature in New York's Hudson Valley. She works with humans who wish to find their center, surrender to mystery, and step into mastery. mindsonfire.org.

KATHY GUIDI is co-creator and steward of Birdsong Retreat & Sanctuary, a place for wellness and spiritual healing in New Zealand. She is a Shamanic Breathwork and women's retreat facilitator, an earth honoring ritualist and apprentice in the Pachakuti Mesa Tradition of Peru, and a spiritual mentor. kathyguidi.com and birdsongretreat.nz.

VICTORIA HANCHIN is a retired Wholistic Psychotherapist, community mentor, and author in Pittsburgh PA, USA. Her passion is to integrate brain neuroscience and quantum physics with ancient spiritual knowledge. She is the author of her memoir *The Seer and The Sayer, Revelations of the New Earth* and has created a brain retraining video available on her website. wholepersonwholeplanet.com.

ROBIN BLAIRE HARMAN is educated in music, ethics, and the arts. She has focused on in-depth consciousness work, including decades with Oscar Miro-Quesada Solevo. She loves chai tea and communing with trees. robinharman.com.

TEMPLE HAYES is a difference maker, global spiritual leader, shamanic energy healer, radio host, and author. She is a sought-after keynote speaker and has spoken to hundreds of thousands globally. She and her wife live in Santa Barbara, CA. templehayes.com.

DEBBIE IRVINE, MCOUN who resides in Australia, traveled to South and North America for spiritual healings. These mystical experiences healed her permanent primary immunodeficiency disease, critical hypertension, and transformed her life. Previously declared Total and Permanently Disabled with ill-health and retired from her musical career, Debbie now practices as a counselor and a shamanic and dreamwork practitioner.

DAVID JORDAN is a sanctioned teacher of the Pachakuti Mesa Tradition and a licensed professional counselor. He holds a Master of Theological Studies degree from Emory University and a Master of Arts in Counseling Psychology from Prescott College. As the owner of Burning Bear Healing Arts, LLC, David is in private practice as an integrated psychotherapist and shamanic practitioner. burningbearhealingarts.com.

ADELE GOODWIN KELEHER is an artist of sacred landscape–listening to the spaces between sounds, sorting patterns, and exploring the portals of human experience. She weaves empowering stories of meaning and grace that incorporate eclectic mysticism, Intentional Creativity, and a career of designing gardens. shamanascape.com.

DEBRA KELLY is a shamanic practitioner and ceremonial facilitator. As an artist of the sacred on the path of the heart, her work in the world is about awakening and the return to Oneness. Practicing ancient healing arts, Debra's medicine brings deep soul remembering and inspires soul transformation. insacredways.com.

ALLISON KENNY is a featured author and contributor for the award-winning publishing division of 360° Nation. Her work explores divine beauty and encounters with the unknown having had a deeply spiritual life and shamanic experiences since she was a child. Allison is the creator of the online course, Bellydance Meditation˙ movement method both live and online. bellydance-meditation.teachable.com.

JUNE KONOPKA does Spiritual Counseling and Hakomi Mindful Somatic Self-Discovery work with individuals interested in integrating our animal, human, and Divine selves in an embodied awakening here on Earth. junekonopka.com.

JUDY LEMON is a shamanic practitioner and certified trauma therapist with a private practice in southern California. She brings her extensive experience and knowledge into her work of helping others to break free of limiting patterns using trauma-informed shamanism. judylemon.com.

F. PIETER LEFFERTS is an artist, earthling, and author of *What The Kek Kek Saw*. Pieter's art is in collections both prominent and humble, far and wide. pieterlefferts.com.

DR. BONNIE MCLEAN is a retired RN and current Acupuncture Physician and Doctor of Oriental Medicine, shamanic healing practitioner, author, and speaker. She was named Top Acupuncturist and Doctor of Oriental

Medicine 2020, Holistic Healer of the Decade, and is a recipient of a Lifetime Achievement Award by IAOTP (International Association of Top Professionals). spiritgatemedicine.com.

ANASTASIA MICHELLE is a yoga teacher who is deeply tuned with Gaia. She hopes to inspire those who feel they are ready to step into their soul's purpose. alunayoga.wordpress.com.

AMANDA MONTOYA is a student of life and dabbles in many things, writing being one. She is a mother of three and currently calls Colorado Springs her home. journeywithyin.com.

MONA RAIN is a sanctioned teacher of the Pachakuti Mesa Tradition, earth steward and ceremonialist for *Gaia-Pachamama*. Humbly and with reverence for all, she shares her healing, teachings, and Peru vision quests. chacarunahealing.com.

REV. STEPHANIE RED FEATHER, PH.D. is a Divine Feminine change agent and award-winning, bestselling author of *The Evolutionary Empath*, creator of Empath Activation Cards, and contributing author to three other bestselling books. bluestartemple.org.

MICHAEL BLUEMOON RIVERON is a shaman and carrier of the Pachakuti Mesa Tradition. Working as a healer he endeavors to follow his dream of becoming an author. soulbodyhealing.net.

DEBORAH SHINING STAR is a shamanic arts practitioner, ceremonialist, bestselling author, and visionary artist. She is a mesa carrier and an initiate of the Andean and coastal lineage traditions of Peru. Her passion is supporting women to align with their soul-full gifts of empowerment through deep, energetic Earth and Shamanic-based practices. deborahshiningstar.com.

SHARON M. SIRKIS, BSN is a Black Belt, accredited T'ai Chi Chih teacher, certified Chakra Energy Healer, firekeeper, and singer for Sundance and Native American sweat lodge ceremonies.

AGUSTINA THORGILSSON'S vision is to help make the world a better place by showing people how to transcend difficult life experiences by using their intuition, insights, and the ancient knowledge known to man. lifenavigation.com.

MEET OUR FEATURED AUTHOR

An international renown kamasqa curandero, altomisayoq adept, and earth-honoring ritualist from Peru, don Oscar Miro-Quesada Solevo is the visionary founder of The Heart Of The Healer (THOTH) Shamanic Mystery School, the originator of Pachakuti Mesa Tradition cross-cultural shamanism, author of Healing Light, and co-author of Lessons in Courage: Peruvian Shamanic Wisdom for Everyday Life. Aside from his extensive personal involvement and scholarly contributions related to the practice of cross-cultural shamanism, don Oscar is a Fellow in Ethnopsychology with the Organization of American States, Invited N.G.O. Observer to the United Nations Permanent Forum on Indigenous Issues, and Founding Counselor of its Inter-Spiritual Dialogue Committee, Acting Member of the Source of Synergy Evolutionary Leaders Circle, and together with Jean Houston, Jack Canfield, Neale Donald Walsch, Ervin Laszlo, Lynne Twist, Rinaldo Brutoco,

Michael Bernard Beckwith, Ashok K. Gangadean, Dot Maver, Lynne McTaggart, and James O'Dea, one of twelve luminaries convened by the late Barbara Marx Hubbard to form on her Birth 2012 Welcoming Committee.

Some of his more mainstream accomplishments include an A.S. degree in Life Sciences/Microbiology from Mitchell College, a B.A. in Psychology with a minor in Comparative Religion from Duke University, an M.A. in Humanistic/Transpersonal Clinical Psychology from West Georgia State University, and a two-year post-masters specialization degree in Ethnopsychology granted by Organization of American States (O.A.S.) fulfilled through the Department of Interdisciplinary Studies at Emory University in Atlanta, Georgia. His research in interdisciplinary studies while at Emory, combined with two years of fieldwork in medical anthropology among Peru's northern coastal and southeastern highland rural populations, led to the creation of indigenous community-based mental health and substance abuse treatment programs in partnership with native folk healers that became integrated into Peru's public health care delivery system at a national level. He has likewise held distinguished appointments in academia, clinical psychology, and healthcare that are far too numerous to mention for this profile page.

Famed for his ritual mastery in Peruvian kamasqa and altomisayoq shamanic lineages, don Oscar's apprenticeship in northern coastal wachuma curanderismo and initiation into the southeastern Andean paqokuna shaman/priesthood formally took place between the years 1969 and 1986. His first immersion into the living soul and mythic reality of Peruvian shamanism was realized under the stern tutelage of the famed wachumero don Celso Rojas Palomino from Salas, a then small agricultural community near the city of Chiclayo. don Oscar accomplished his apprenticeship in northern coastal curanderismo fulfilling the dual role of auxilio de mesada ("medicine lodge"/ "healing altar auxiliary" or "ritual assistant") and rastrero ("clairvoyant diagnostician"/ "diviner"), eventually becoming don Celso's segundo de mando en banco ("second in command for curing sessions"). This intensely demanding apprenticeship process transpired during the winter months (June, July, and August in the Southern Hemisphere) each year until don Celso's untimely passing in July of 1982.

Less than a month after this sorrowful event, don Oscar found himself serendipitously involved in a considerably less formal, more sporadic four-year apprenticeship within the southeastern Andean Paqo tradition of shamanism with famed kuraq akulleq don Benito Corihuaman Vargas from the village of Wasao, a farming community one hour south of Cusco. In recognition of his expeditious grasp of traditional Q'eswaruna cosmovision, witnessed through the skilled performance of traditional propitiatory earth-honoring ceremonies, don Oscar received his musqochiwarqa qallariy transmission as altomisayoq from don Benito in November of 1985, barely seven months before this deeply revered elder also made his passing in June of 1986.

He is a popular faculty member at The Shift Network and educational centers in the USA and abroad, dedicating his life to the revitalization of aboriginal wisdom traditions as a means of restoring sacred trust between humankind and the natural world. Oscar has been facilitating experiential workshops and apprenticeship series of workshops that integrate millennial and contemporary healing practices and Earth-honoring ceremonial traditions with a focus on the creation of heartfelt sacred communities around the world since 1979. He has been leading exemplary cross-cultural shamanic apprenticeship expeditions to sacred sites of the world since 1986. His widely acclaimed ethnospiritual pilgrimages to ancestral lands are masterfully orchestrated to inspire a life of reverence and eco-restorative relationship with our beloved *Pachamama* ("Earth Mother") as a destined part of our human identity as an Earth-honoring global family.

Aside from his currently established regional apprenticeship series in the U.S.A. and Europe, he has also been a popular teacher at prestigious international centers of leading-edge education such as Naropa, Shambhala Mountain Center, Interface, New York Open Center, Rowe, Frankfurter-Ring, Omega, and Esalen, to name a few. A seasoned navigator of non-ordinary states of consciousness, don Oscar is well prepared to help people from all walks of life access realms of Being through which multidimensional powers and forces are available for healing self, others, and our planetary ecosystem. His ceremonial work and shamanic apprenticeship programs have been featured on Sounds True, CNN, Univision, A&E, Discovery Channel and The History Channel's Ancient Aliens.

More important than all the credentials is that don Oscar is a warm, loving human being who deeply cares about people and our planet and has an infectious belly laugh. He is a master at creating sacred community using the magic of joy, love, and compassion as the strands that gently weave us together as a planetary family. His deep caring for each student is expressed in his keen attention to life-transforming ceremonial detail and group healing dynamics within each sacred hoop he's called to serve. In essence, don Oscar's life is best described as "transforming the world through sacred living," as he lovingly carries forth a pragmatic vision of global human spiritual awakening based on the co-creation of sustainable earth-honoring sacred communities worldwide.

"When we surrender the need to figure it all out and cultivate the ability to let it all in, our earth walk becomes a sacred dance of healing service on the planet. More than the world needs saving; it needs loving."

—don Oscar

Learn more at www.theheartofthehealer.org.

Printed in Great Britain
by Amazon